KU-307-855

Follow This Thread

Follow This Thread
A Maze Book to Get Lost In

HENRY ELIOT

Illustrated by Quibe

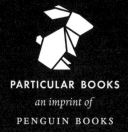

PARTICULAR BOOKS

an imprint of

PENGUIN BOOKS

DÚN LAOGHAIRE-
RATHDOWN LIBRARIES

DLR27000019462	
BERTRAMS	22/08/2018
GE	02348871

ouse

at

First published 2018

001

Copyright © Henry Eliot, 2018

Illustrations copyright © Quibe, 2018

The moral right of the author has been asserted

Designed by Jim Stoddart

Set in Garamond 12.5 pt and Baskerville MT 24 pt

Printed in Italy by L.E.G.O. S.p.A.

A CIP catalogue record for this book is available
from the British Library

ISBN: 978-1-846-14931-3

www.greenpenguin.co.uk

MIX
Paper from
responsible sources
FSC® C018179

Penguin Books is committed to a sustainable
future for our business, our readers and our
planet. This book is made from paper certified
by the Forest Stewardship Council.

For TK & GG

The crescent moon traces the horns
of Gugalanna, the Bull of Heaven . . .

...who also survives in the constellation
Taurus, where his red giant of an eye glints
between lowered horns.

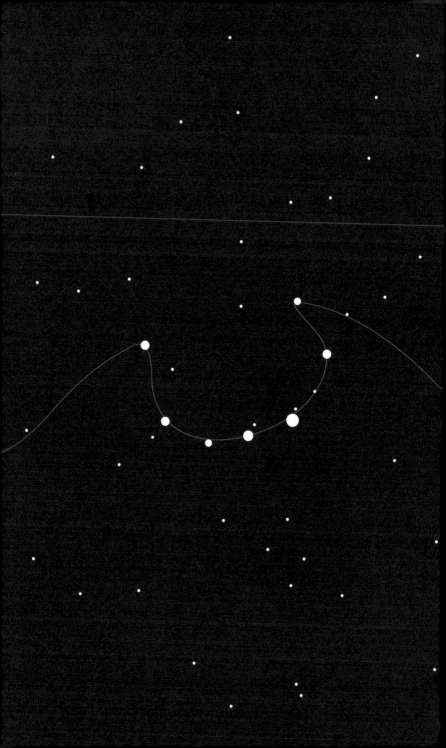

Midway upon the journey of our life
I found myself within a forest dark,
For the straightforward pathway had been lost.

—Dante

Mouth

At Cumae, west of Naples, a headland of volcanic tuff breaches the sea.

It is honeycombed with interconnecting caves and corridors, passages that coil and twist down into the bowels of the earth. It was here the Sibyl sang for a thousand years, unable to die, and it was through these subterranean entrails that Aeneas picked his way to the Land of the Dead.

Above ground, the bluff is topped by an acropolis: temple columns reaching up to the heavens and the sun god Apollo. The sky is closer here than in other places: the air's invisible currents, thermals and fly-lines converge above Cumae.

Amongst the clouds there is a bird, too distant to make out clearly. Its flight is clumsy as it approaches, its tattered wings barely holding the thin air. The lumbering creature flip-flops out of the sky and lands in a tangled mess of sticks and feathers on the beach. A man crawls free of the wreckage. He has flown more than a thousand miles with arms strapped to artificial wings.

Broken, he limps along the sand, looking for shelter from the wrathful sun. He has watched his only son plummet through fathoms of air to puncture the stony waves. A partridge chuckles as he passes.

Finding a cool crevice in the rock, one of the earth's hundred entries at Cumae, he collapses into the mouth of a cave.

In 1956, another man entered the caves at Cumae.

Michael Ayrton, sculptor, metal-founder and draughts-man, was holidaying in Italy when he was 'god-struck' by the myth of Daedalus, the master craftsman who built himself wings and flew from Crete to Cumae. 'The legend grew in me,' Ayrton wrote, 'forced itself upon me and emerged in the form of reliefs, bronzes, drawings and paintings'.

Increasingly, Ayrton identified with Daedalus. He wrote *The Testament of Daedalus* and later *The Maze Maker*, both fictional autobiographies, and he was the first man since Daedalus to cast a real honeycomb out of solid gold. He achieved this feat by plaster casting a honeycomb, melting the natural wax away and building a centrifuge to spin the liquid metal into the impossibly thin crevices. Seventeen prototypes broke, spangling his Essex workshop with molten gold.

Ayrton's fascination with Daedalus resurrected an inter-est in the art of maze making. Three decades earlier, William Henry Matthews had been pessimistic about the longevity of the maze: 'With regard to its future develop-ments,' he wrote in *Mazes and Labyrinths: A General Account of Their History and Developments*, '[. . .] we could not hope to sound an expectant note without creating an impression of fatuity.'

Today there are more mazes in the world than ever before, and more being constructed every year. 'It is no overstatement,' writes the maze maker Adrian Fisher, 'to say that we are living through the greatest Golden Age of mazes.'

But mazes are not comfortable places. The entrance to The Forbidden Corner maze garden in North Yorkshire, for example, is an animatronic monster's mouth, which burps and wiggles its fleshy uvula as you're swallowed along its gullet. A maze is disconcerting, specifically designed to wrong-foot you, to scatter your bearings. As a rule, we take care not to get lost, so why should we willingly enter a maze?

Why was Alice 'burning' to step into the rabbit-hole?

When Daedalus regained his strength, he set about building a temple at Cumae, dedicated to Apollo. He offered his oar-like wings as propitiation, hanging them high above the altar.

He designed a pair of gates for the temple, in bronze, and cast them with reliefs, crafting his own story across their metalled surface as on to the pages of a book.

He depicts King Minos of Crete, praying to Poseidon to sanction his kingship with a worthy sacrifice. In answer, the god sends Minos a gleaming white bull trotting out of the waves.

6

The beast is spectacular. It is so impressive, in fact, that Minos chooses a common ox to sacrifice instead, and looses the white bull amongst his herd of sacred cows.

But Poseidon is insulted and takes revenge: the loins of Queen Pasiphae, Minos's wife, are seized with an unnatural, uncontrollable lust for the white bull.

Her nagging desire grows unbearable until she begs relief from a foreigner at the palace: Daedalus. In secret, he builds her a wicker cow, hollow and lifelike, into which she is strapped after nightfall, and in this way the snorting bull is able to mount the pleasure-hungry queen and quench her.

Not long afterwards, Pasiphae feels her womb begin to stir. A strange fruit starts to grow; the trap is sprung.

Trap

The screams have stopped.

Daedalus hurries along chiaroscuro corridors, his face glowing in the light thrown by spitting tapers. The route to the royal bedchamber is convoluted: across marble courtyards, down intricate galleries and narrow passages, up broad stone stairwells. At last he arrives at the heart of the palace, and knocks at the queen's door.

Pasiphae lies unconscious on twisted sheets. Minos stands grim and motionless. Nearby, a midwife is weeping, and from a hooded crib comes a puffing, snuffling sound that Daedalus can't place.

He catches Minos's eye and steps gingerly towards the cradle. The candlelight is dim, and he has to peer closely to be sure he's not mistaken. Surely the gods could not be this cruel. 'His name will be Asterion, the Star-Child,' says Minos, standing beside him. 'You, Daedalus, are responsible for this monster.'

Daedalus's punishment is his greatest commission: he is to design and construct a nursery for Asterion, a house with many rooms and many doors, a house that is easy to enter but impossible to leave, a house that is both a shrine to a demi-god and an oubliette, a house in which Minos can shut his bull-headed bastard and never see him again.

A house for the Minotaur.

A maze is a structure that connects the external world to its internal world, and yet remains inextricable.

Some people draw a distinction between a labyrinth and a maze: a labyrinth has one convoluted, looping path and no choices, whereas a maze has forked paths, wrong turns and dead ends. The difference is historical as well as structural: labyrinths were scratched into rocks as early as 4,500 years ago, but the earliest surviving maze design is barely 600 years old.

The unicursal seven-path labyrinth pattern may have been inspired by fingerprint whorls, by the bounded chaos of corals, by spiral shells, by the apparent track of the planet Mercury, by the breathing anatomy of whales, which Melville calls a 'labyrinth of vermicelli-like vessels', by sliced cabbages, exposed brains or spilled divinatory guts. The remarkable fact is how widespread it is: variations on the same pattern were used by early cultures across Europe, Africa, Asia and the Americas.

Mazes, on the other hand, evolved just as Europe was transitioning out of the Middle Ages into the Renaissance, from a world governed by the will of God, in which the single thread of one's predetermined life was already spun, to a new world of free will and personal choice, in which man was both the author and the hero of his life story.

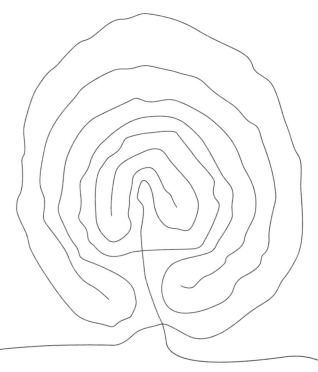

The differences can be distracting, however. Like Cretan drachmas, which displayed the Minotaur on one side and the labyrinth symbol on the other, labyrinths and mazes are two sides of the same coin: the figurative single thread representing the true path through a complex maze.

The Labyrinth that Daedalus designed for the Minotaur was a maze.

It was 'krynkeled to and fro' says Chaucer. It was 'not only a maze in plan but a maze in depth, so that paths doubled back above themselves and twisted below each other'. This is how Michael Ayrton imagines it in *The Maze Maker*. 'Steps and ramps sharply or gently ascending and descending occurred as frequently as horizontal passages.'

Designing a maze requires an array of topological techniques, and for six centuries we have been reassembling Daedalus's methods, recovering his hidden principles of maze making. The earliest surviving maze is in the Bavarian Staatsbibliothek in Munich, in a book of early fifteenth-century technical drawings by a Venetian magus called Giovanni Fontana.

This remarkable volume, known as the *Bellicorum Instrumentorum Liber*, 'the book of war machines', is mostly filled with pictures of bizarre weapons: mechanical camels, exploding globes, fire cannon, rocket-propelled rabbits and violent helter-skelters. On facing pages Fontana includes two maze designs, one circular and one square. No earlier mazes are known to exist.

In Fontana's commentary, he explains that he was inspired by Daedalus to draw these two-dimensional designs with 'laborious paths, dark, winding convolutions, terrors, loops and lonely places'. Given the number of aggressive contraptions that fill the book, he clearly envisaged them as traps: either defensive walls for protecting a citadel, or more likely cruel dungeons for driving one's enemies insane.

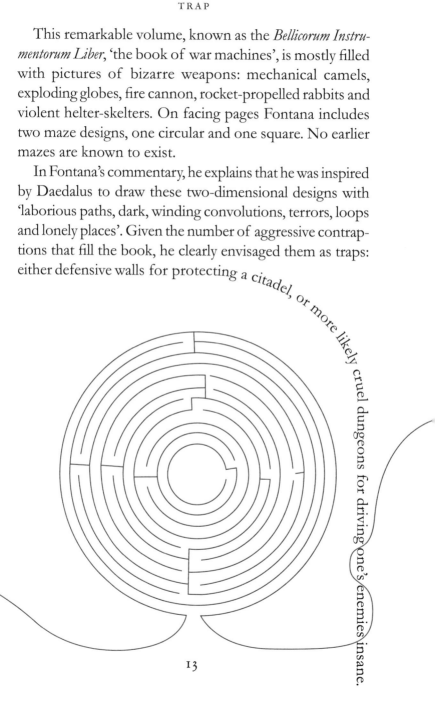

The idea of the maze caught on and was adopted by garden designers across Europe, who played down the claustrophobia and focused on the delight a puzzle maze could afford a formal garden.

The Hôtel des Tournelles in Paris had a 'labyrinth, called the house of Daedalus', as early as 1431, and in 1477 King René renovated a hedge maze at the Château de Baugé in Anjou.

One of history's grandest and most popular garden mazes was the labyrinth at Versailles, laid out for Louis XIV, the Sun King, in 1674. This maze consisted of dense foliage carved through with a relatively simple network of paths. The fabulist Charles Perrault advised on its layout, installing decorative fountains at each junction, allowing the visitor to lose herself 'agréablement'.

'A Labyrinth is a Place cut into several Windings, set off with Horn-beam, to divide them one from the other,' wrote George London and Henry Wise, two contemporary English gardeners. '[T]he most valuable Labyrinths are always those that wind most, as that of Versailles, the Contrivance of which has been wonderfully lik'd by all that have seen it.'

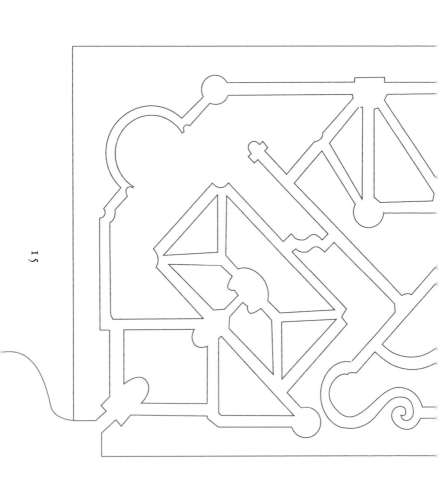

London and Wise attempted to improve on the contrivance at Versailles when they designed their own maze for the new King of England, William of Orange.

The Hampton Court Maze is the oldest surviving hedge maze in Britain and probably the most famous in the world. In 2016, 160,000 visitors pitted their wits against this 300-year-old puzzle. The maze is wedged into a corner of the palace's 'wilderness', and has a distinctive trapezoid shape. As a result,

the path has almost no right angles, which makes it particularly hard to orientate yourself inside: trying to use the nearby gatepost lions as a fixed point of reference, for example, proves futile.

Its excessive popularity has taken its toll, unfortunately. The path is tarmacked, the hedges are ragged in places and the pair of trees that once marked the centre ha

sappeared, but the ingenious design continues to baffle visitors.

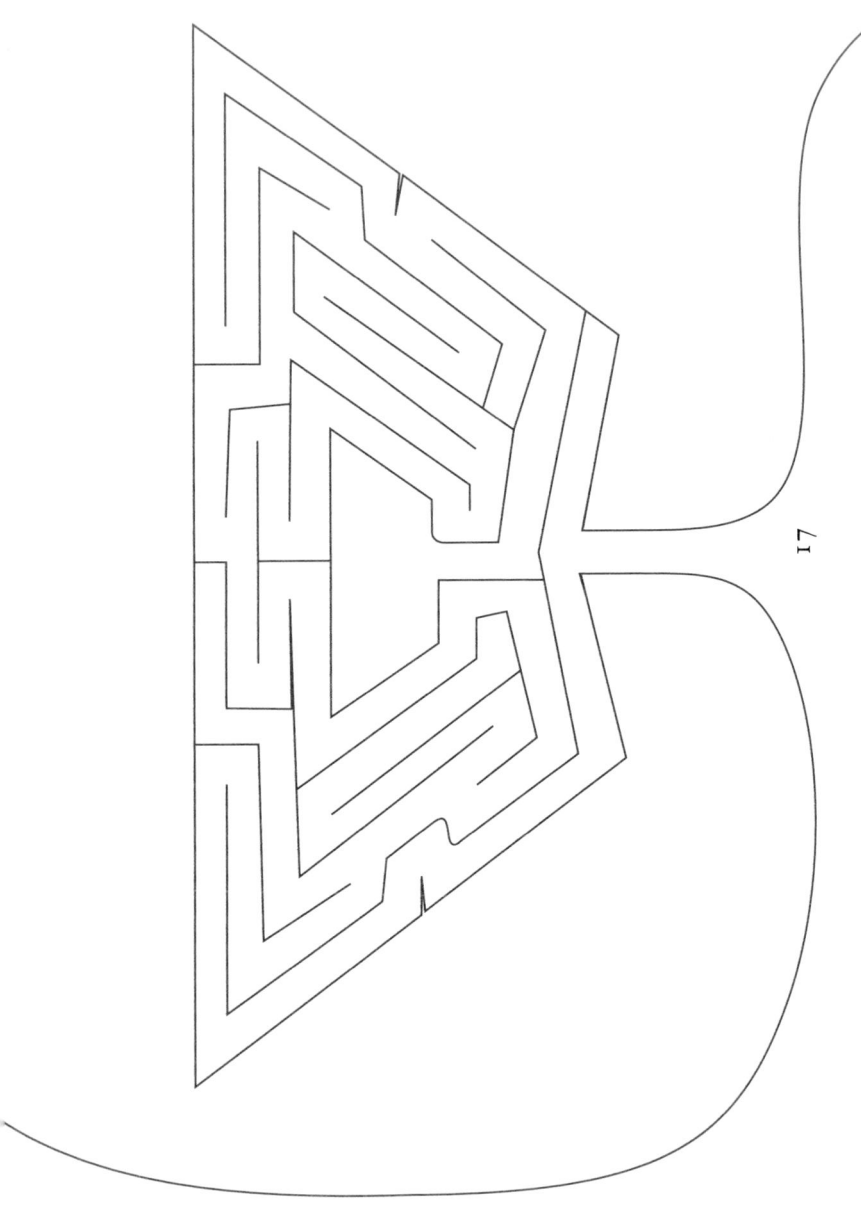

'It's absurd to call it a maze,' says Harris in Jerome K. Jerome's *Three Men in a Boat*. 'You keep on taking the first turning to the right.'

Once inside, however, Harris discovers that the Hampton Court Maze is harder to solve than he imagined. He confidently gathers a group of lost visitors and eventually leads them to the centre, but every time he tries to lead them out again, they end up back in the middle. Increasingly desperate, they call a young maze keeper who comes in to fetch them, but he's new to the job and becomes hopelessly lost himself.

If Harris had stuck to his guns, his technique should have worked: if you enter and keep your right (or left) hand in contact with the right-hand (or left-hand) wall at all times, following the hedge wherever it takes you, including in and out of dead ends, you will eventually reach the centre. It works on the way out as well.

It's not the quickest way to the goal (the shortest formula is to turn left when you enter, then right, right again, left, left, left and finally left), but the 'hand-on-wall' method works because most of the hedges in the Hampton Court Maze are connected to each other; crucially, the hedge around the central goal is connected to the maze's external boundary hedge. This means that if you maintain contact with the wall throughout, you are bound to reach the centre.

This method is painstaking but infallible when applied to any maze planted before the early nineteenth century.

As a teenager in the 1820s, Philip Henry Stanhope was commissioned by his father to design a maze for their family estate at Chevening in Kent. In the process he uncovered the first principle of advanced maze design.

Inspired by his great-grandfather, the mathematician and second Earl Stanhope, he included a number of free-standing hedges within his maze: the masterstroke was for one of these 'island' hedges to cocoon the maze's goal, disconnecting the centre from the boundary hedge.

Maze islands flummox anyone attempting the hand-on-wall method: if you keep your hand in contact with the hedge as you enter, you eventually return to the entrance without ever having reached the middle. To get to the goal, at some point you need to let go and strike out into the unknown.

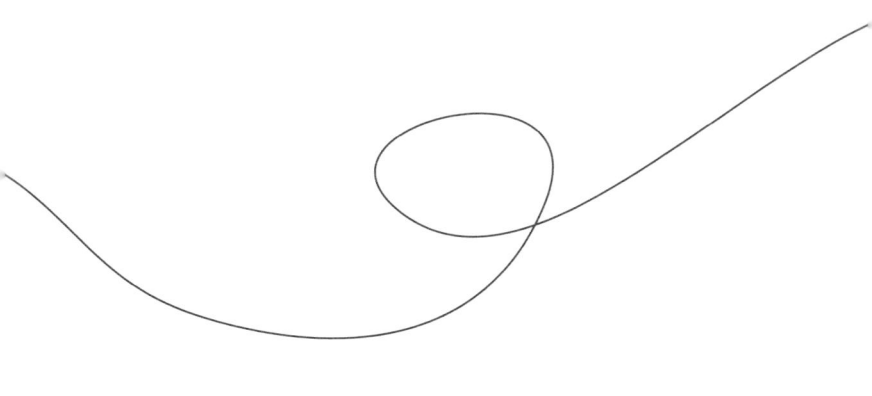

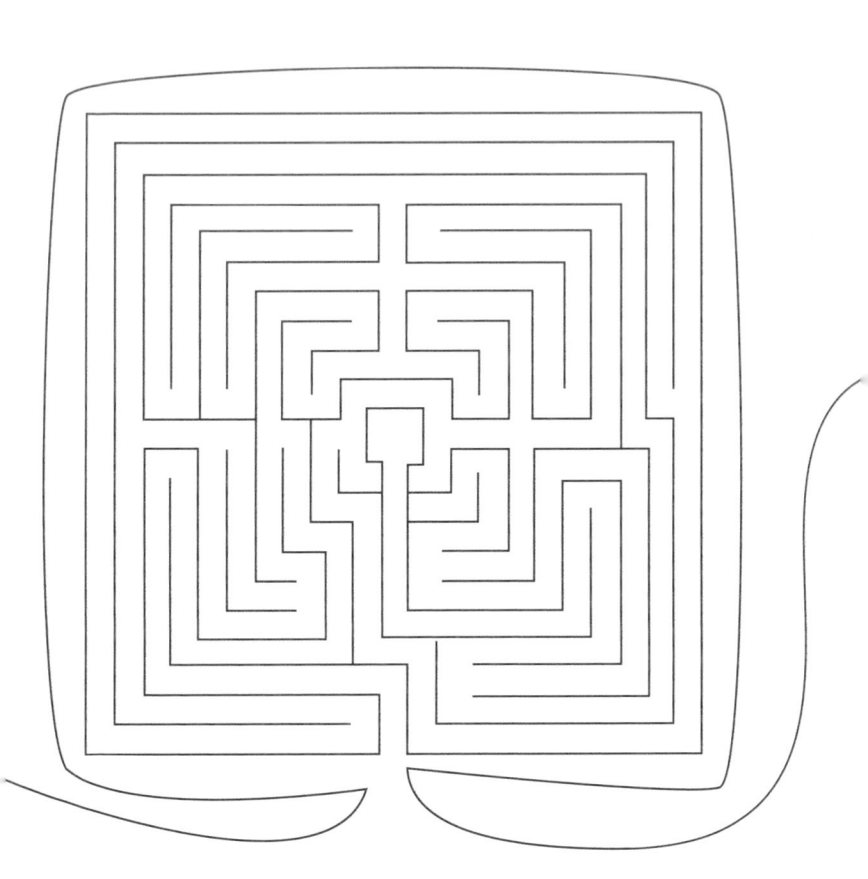

Philip Henry's ground-breaking design still survives, although Chevening House is now the official residence of the UK's Foreign Secretary and the maze is not usually accessible to the public.

A new method for solving mazes was required, and the French mathematician Charles Pierre Trémaux lent his name to the procedure, which he published in 1882.

William of Baskerville summarizes 'Trémaux's Algorithm' in Umberto Eco's *The Name of the Rose*:

'To find the way out of a labyrinth [. . .] there is only one means. At every new junction, never seen before, the path we have taken will be marked with three signs. If, because of previous signs on some of the paths of the junction, you see that the junction has already been visited, you will make only one mark on the path you have taken. If all the apertures have already been marked, then you must retrace your steps. But if one or two apertures of the junction are still without signs, you will choose any one, making two signs on it. Proceeding through an aperture that bears only one sign, you will make two more, so that now the aperture bears three. All the parts of the labyrinth must have been visited if, arriving at a junction, you never take a passage with three signs, unless none of the other passages is now without signs.'

'And by observing this rule you get out?' asks the novice Adso.

'Almost never, as far as I know', replies William.

Islands greatly increase the complexity of a maze. Five further principles of maze design have since been developed, four of them the brainchild of one man, known as 'the Maze King'.

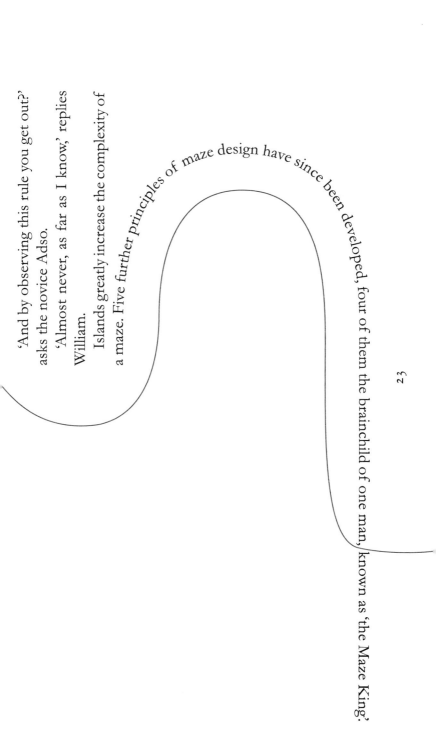

'In 1971 something hit me. I went out like a rabid mole and began digging myself a maze.'

Headliners at the Glastonbury Free Festival in 1971 included David Bowie, Fairport Convention and The Worthy Farm Windfuckers. Michael Eavis, dairy farmer and founder of the Glastonbury Festival, remembers how once the 'freaks and hippies' had dispersed, the debris had been cleared away and the newly installed pyramid stage stood empty, one man remained in his field: a nineteen-year-old with waist-length golden hair called Greg Bright.

Bright asked whether Eavis had a spare acre or two of land he could use to dig a maze.

'He looked at me as if I was crazy,' Bright wrote later, 'but he let me have a field that was too wet for his cows. He expected me to camp there a couple of weeks and then leave.'

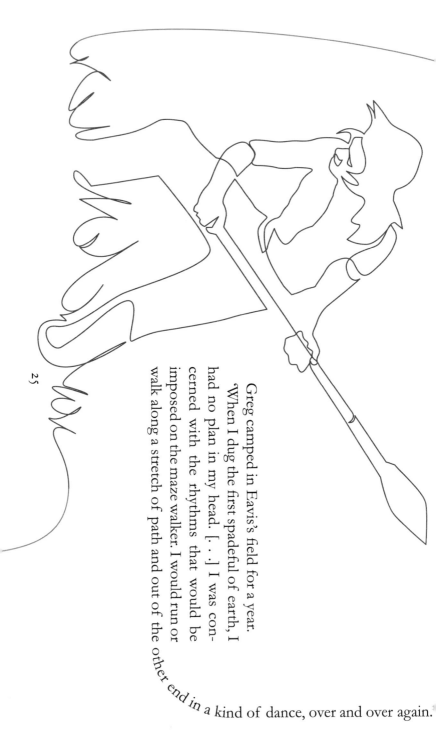

Greg camped in Eavis's field for a year. 'When I dug the first spadeful of earth, I had no plan in my head. [..] I was concerned with the rhythms that would be imposed on the maze walker. I would run or walk along a stretch of path and out of the other end in a kind of dance, over and over again.'

After two months, Greg had a design marked out that covered approximately two-thirds of an acre, and he set to work deepening the trenches. The depths varied: some paths were as shallow as eighteen inches; others were six feet deep. It was back-breaking work that riddled his palms with calluses. He fought a constant battle against wasps, pooling water and rampant vegetation. At one point he laid waste the entire field, scorching every living thing with toxic viologen salts. On wet days he would shelter inside his tent and draw elaborate mazes in a black leather notebook, puncturing the paper with a charred chopstick so that the paths could spill across multiple pages.

'A vole lived under my tent where he dug a labyrinth of his own,' he remembered. 'I think the stoat got him.'

Greg discovered a new principle of maze design while working on his maze at Worthy Farm in Pilton.

He imagined it as a collection of smaller mazes, connected at nodal junctions he called 'mutually accessible centres'.

Mutually accessible centres convert a maze into a network, like a city underground system: the accessible centres are the interchanges, and discrete sections of the maze are the connecting lines.

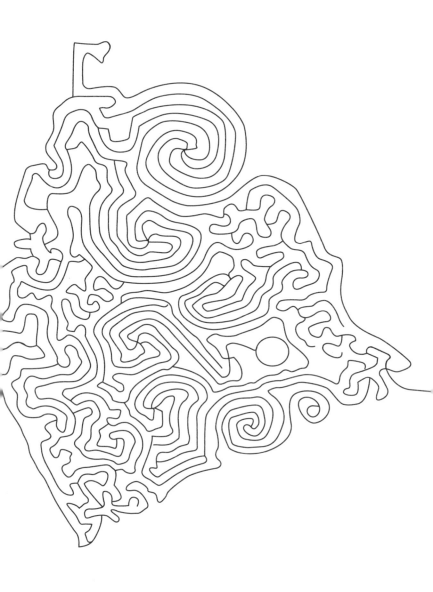

Each time you move from one section of the maze to another, you might be progressing towards the centre, but you might equally be looping back the way you came. Greg thought of mutually accessible centres as keeping the whole maze 'alive at all times'. Put another way, they present the horrific possibility of circling indefinitely, never finding either the centre or the way out.

Worse still, it's only possible to spot these nodal points from a bird's-eye view. From within the maze there is no way of knowing when you've passed from one section to another. Only failing light and mounting déjà vu will tell you you're trapped.

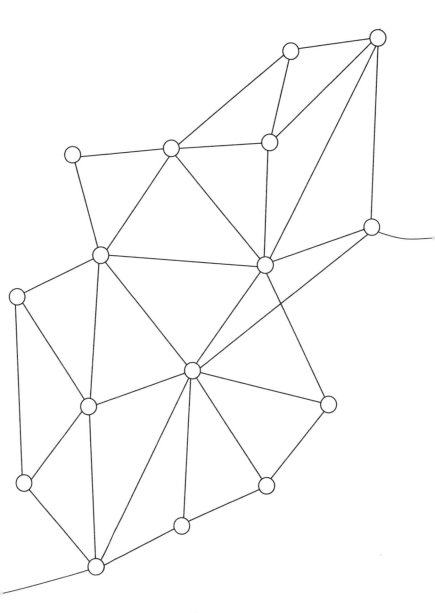

Greg had created what Umberto Eco terms the 'rhizome' labyrinth.

A rhizome is the common rootstock of spreading plants such as grasses, bamboos and poplar trees. Instead of individual, branching root structures, a rhizome is one single, connected mass, any two points of which may be connected in multiple ways. A labyrinth of this kind 'promises us a network whose path can always provide us with new ways', Eco writes; '[. . .] we have the impression that we can never exit'.

In 'The Library of Babel', the Argentine author and librarian Jorge Luis Borges imagines a rhizomic universe: a network of hexagonal galleries, stretching away in all directions. Each gallery contains 20 bookshelves; each shelf contains 35 books; each book has 410 pages; and the books contain every possible permutation of letters.

In the story, traveller-librarians pass from gallery to gallery, searching for a legendary circular book with a continuous spine, a catalogue of catalogues that will explain the mysteries of this strange world. The narrator eventually realizes, however, that the library has what Einstein called 'spherical geometry': it is cyclical in every direction. Travelling forwards eventually returns you to the hexagon from which you set out, without having passed more than a negligible fraction of the total number of books above and below you.

'Could there be a matrix of the universe?' wonders Greg expansively in one of his maze books. 'It is both finite and unbounded.'

Greg called his next principle of maze design 'partial valves'. These are the most distinctive feature of his mazes. Consisting of three or more paths that twist and swirl around each other, they resemble whirlpools, cyclones or spiralling galaxies.

Walkers enter these spirals and emerge into a central clearing, the 'eye' of the spiral, where they are faced with a choice of onward paths. Whichever path the walker chooses, there is a statistical probability she will struggle to retrace her footsteps, because on returning to the centre of the spiral it is hard to remember from which path she originally entered.

In this way these spirals act as valves in the maze system: privileging movement from one section to another, and restricting movement in the opposite direction. They are effective with three paths; Greg's preference was for five.

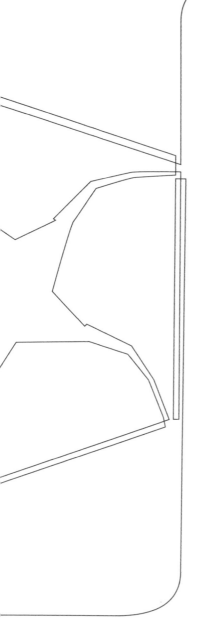

Greg thought of partial valves as a way to 'control tides of movement' within his mazes. Duck decoys work in the same way. These netted, hooped structures were built over artificial ditches of water, and were once common across England and the Netherlands.

Ducks are naturally inquisitive birds and trappers would exploit their innate curiosity,

using a small water spaniel to lead them into the mouth of the decoy, while they hid behind screens arranged at angles along the curved ditch. Once the ducks passed the first screen, they saw the first trapper and, scared, paddled further. Each screen revealed a new trapper until the terrified ducks paddled all the way to the end of the tapering pipe, into the trappers' sack and a literal dead end.

Eel bucks, lobster pots and wasp traps have similar one-way designs. In Sicily, the annual *mattanza* tuna harvest involved laying a maze of netted 'rooms', connected by valves, two or three miles out to sea. Fish would gradually penetrate the system until they arrived at the final *camera della morte*, the 'chamber of death'. When this final room was full, the nets would be raised to the surface by *tonnare* boats and fishermen bludgeoned the gasping fish to death.

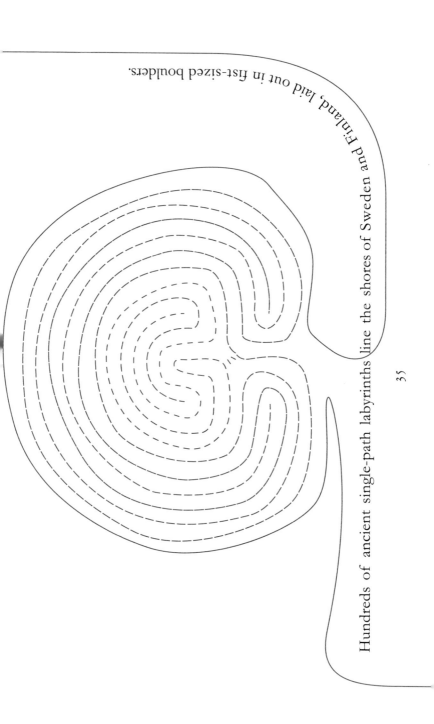

Hundreds of ancient single-path labyrinths line the shores of Sweden and Finland, laid out in fist-sized boulders.

Superstitious fishermen used these labyrinths as supernatural decoys. Running through a labyrinth tempts the wicked *smågubbar*, the little people, to follow you inside. Traditionally, evil spirits travel only in straight lines, so luring them into the labyrinth leaves them trapped while you cast out to sea, hoping for a good day's catch before they escape and whip up the bad weather.

As recently as 1955, a fisherman was seen running a labyrinth on the rocky Swedish promontory of Kuggören, which juts into the Gulf of Bothnia. He was spitting on his hand as he ran, throwing the spittle over his shoulder to distract the *smågubbar* close at his heels.

In ancient Rome, labyrinths were placed adjacent to thresholds as spirit traps, and today in southern India you can see protective labyrinths traced in rice flour on doorsteps. In Scotland 'tangled threids' were once marked in pipeclay on barn doors and the floors of byres, invoking the charm:

> *Tangled threid and rowan seed*
> *Gar the witches lowse their speed.*

One day a bullock stumbled into Greg's maze at Pilton and became stuck in the mud, tossing its horns, eyes swivelling. Greg ran up to the farm where Michael Eavis had just sat down to lunch, and together they returned and surveyed the stricken beast, which was growing despondent, its muzzle sagging, spluttering in the ditch water. It wasn't a dairy cow so it must have wandered over from a neighbouring farm.

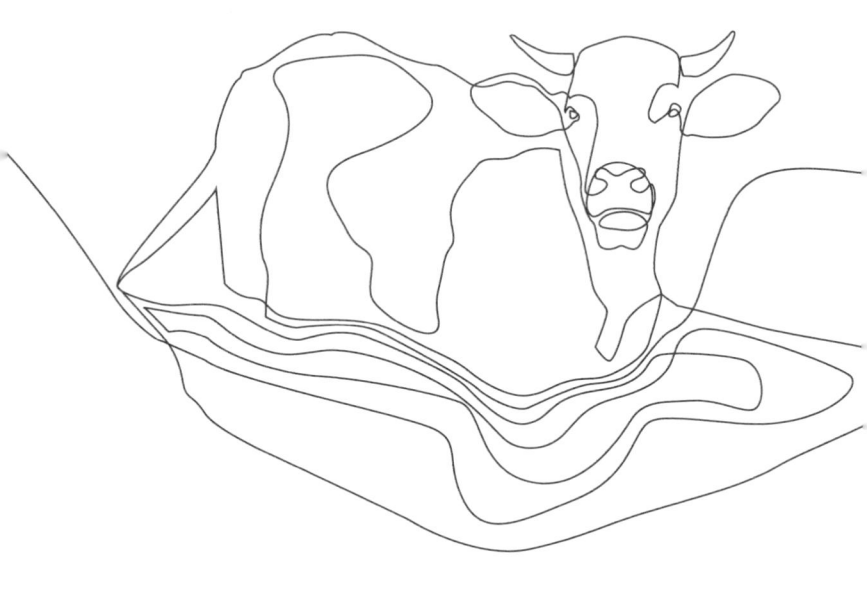

damaged horn and transported the beast to Bruton to be slaughtered for pet food.

Eavis went to fetch a tractor, while Greg crouched down in the maze, supporting the young bull's head and speaking in a soothing voice, looking into its round, bovine eye. 'If the blind lead the blind, both shall fall into the ditch,' grumbled Eavis, turning the tractor, jumping down and looping a thick rope around the bull's horns. The other end he hitched to the machine, and began to ease the tyres forwards, taking the strain. The bull's neck stretched upwards and its eyes widened. Suddenly, one of its horns snapped off at the base, leaving a bloody disc on the skull. Cursing, Eavis tried again, looping the rope under the bull's chin and around its neck. This time, pulled by the umbilical rope, the bullock lurched out of the poachy clay with a loud sucking sound. It scrambled up the bank and staggered to its feet. Eavis unhooked the rope and smacked its flank to herd it away.

When Greg asked after the bullock a few days later, he *learned its owner had claimed insurance for the*

"'Alas," said the mouse, "the world is growing smaller every day. At first it was so big that I was afraid, I ran on and I was glad when at last I saw walls to left and right of me in the distance, but these long walls are closing in on each other so fast that I have already reached the end room, and there in the corner stands the trap that I am heading for."

"You only have to change direction," said the cat, and ate it up.'

Franz Kafka's 'Little Fable' expands the drama of the animal trap to encompass the claustrophobia of the human condition: we fear a featureless world without bound-aries, so we impose structure on our world, but boundaries soon become unbearably constricting, and just as we realize we've walked ourselves into a trap, death catches up with us.

Constricting walls remind us of the limits of our own existence, but the difference in a maze is that it offers the prospect of redemption. There is the possibility of achieving the goal at the centre, turning around and emerging again.

We walk into a maze defiantly, pitting ourselves against both the maze and the maze maker, hoping to prove ourselves in the quest.

Quest

A yellow mouth gobbles biscuits, pursued by ghosts called Blinky, Pinky, Inky and Clyde.

You are a space marine battling an invasion of demons from Hell and negotiating a labyrinthine military base on the Martian moon Phobos.

A chesty action hero in micro-shorts slays mutants and solves puzzles as she fights through a series of underground mazes to

Video games were quick to capitalize on the challenge inherent in mazes. Riddling corridors provide an ideal setting for a virtual hero. The first maze game appeared in 1973: *Gotcha* was a two-player arcade game set in an on-screen maze, the walls of which were in constant motion. The pursuer controlled a square, chasing the other player's plus sign. A constant electronic beeping grew louder and more frequent as the gap between the two symbols narrowed, until the square finally caught the plus sign and it was wiped off the screen.

The manufacturers called it a 'pell-mell "Cat and Mouse" game [. . .] with loads of challenges and excitement [. . .] plenty of psychological twists and turns, and free-flowing adrenalin'.

43

All mazes are games of cat and mouse, played between the maze maker and the maze walker. The maker plays his cards up front, challenging the walker to negotiate his design; walkers accept the challenge by entering the maze and attempting to solve it.

When the stakes are low, mazes are brainteasers. In the sixteenth century, for example, the Paduan sculptor Francesco Segala produced a playful *Libro dei Labirinti* with figurative paper maze puzzles including a prancing jester, a ten-legged crab, a sailing ship and a snail.

Things get more interesting when a time limit is imposed. In 1967, Alan Fletcher installed tiled mazes on the Victoria Line platforms at Warren Street Station in London. These mazes are designed to take four minutes to solve, just longer than the average three-minute wait between tube trains.

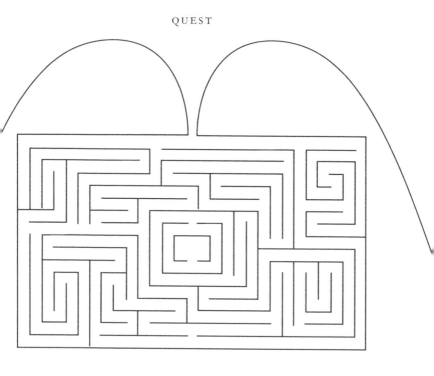

In the traditional Zulu game of *tshuma sogexe*, the head-to-head quality is particularly evident: one boy draws a maze in the sand, with two goals, one of which is identified as the 'royal hut'. He challenges a friend to use a grass stem to trace the correct route to the royal hut. If the second boy makes a mistake or arrives at the wrong hut, the first shouts '*Wapuka sogexe!*' 'You are lost in the labyrinth!'

In the *Aeneid*, Virgil describes the Lusus Troiae, the 'Game of Troy', which was played in Rome in the first centuries CE and BCE.

The Game of Troy was not really a game; it was an equestrian display, performed by young Roman aristocrats at state funerals. It had been devised, according to Virgil, by the hero Aeneas and his band of Trojans.

This military display of intricate horsemanship was supposed to imitate the coils of the Labyrinth.

As once in Crete, the lofty mountain-isle,
That fabled labyrinthine gallery
Wound on through lightless walls, with thousand paths
Which baffled every clue, and led astray
In unreturning mazes dark and blind:
So did the sons of Troy their courses weave
In mimic flights and battles fought for play.

The challenge of the Lusus Troiae was to demonstrate one's skill, precision and bravery within the tight restrictions of the labyrinth pattern. In Rome, as in Pac-Man, the maze was the proving ground for would-be heroes.

One would-be hero sits alone in the sand, drawing patterns.

He is the grandson of King Pittheus of Troizen. He belongs to the royal household, and yet still he sees eyes averted, smirks wiped away, laughter quickly stifled. He knows the joke: how Poseidon lay with his mother on the island of Sphairia and then disappeared into the sea. Once he believed that story; now he wishes his real father hadn't abandoned him and his mother.

He sits alone in the Grove of Zeus, beside a massive weather-scarred altar stone. The stone is another joke: before his father disappeared, he is supposed to have left tokens beneath this great slab, if only it could be lifted. The boy knows from experience it's impossible.

But today, as he doodles in the sand, he has an idea. He has watched the engineers working on the palace walls: he knows their machines, gears and pulleys. Jumping to his feet, he drags a stout pole into the grove and scouts around for a fulcrum.

He works the pole under the stone, uses it as a lever, and yes, incredibly, the great rock begins to heave a few inches into the air. He jams his end below a root, runs back, lies down and reaches underneath. At full stretch he feels nothing, but then his fingers find the edge of a shallow pit and he's just able to reach inside.

A pair of jewelled sandals and a finely wrought sword. The sword bears the serpentine seal of the Erectheids, the royal house of Athens, and below the hilt, inscribed on the blade, his own name: Theseus.

Theseus's mortal father, King Aegeus, left this test for his unborn son: if Theseus could move the rock through strength or wit, he should join his father; if not, he was better off remaining in Troizen, safe from the backstabbing politics of Athens.

This was Theseus's call to arms. Instead of sailing, he set out along the notoriously dangerous Isthmus road.

In the British Museum there is a two-handled *kylix* cup, made in the fifth century BCE, which illustrates the series of labours that Theseus dispatched along the road to Athens, in emulation of his hero Heracles.

First he slew Periphetes the Club-Bearer and kept his deadly iron club. Then he met Sinis the Pine-Bender, who tied his victims to two straining trees until they were ripped apart. His third labour was to grapple with Phaea, the vicious Crommyonian sow. Next he killed Sciron the Corinthian, who would kick strangers into the sea to be devoured by a monstrous turtle. He tackled Cercyon the Arcadian wrestler, and then Procrustes, a psychotic individual, who would invite weary travellers to sleep in his bed and then either hammer them flat if they were short or saw off their limbs if they were tall.

Theseus's final feat was to brave the fire-breathing white bull of Marathon. This great beast had been ravaging the countryside, killing anyone who came close, but Theseus managed to seize it by the horns and lead it through the streets of Athens, driving it up the steep path of the acropolis and sacrificing it to Apollo.

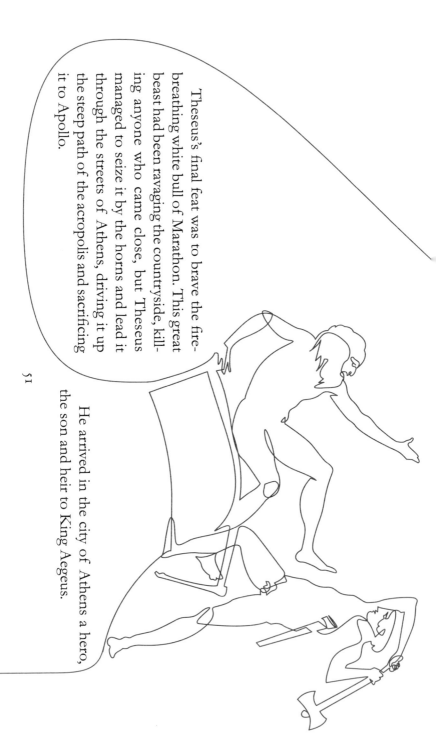

He arrived in the city of Athens a hero, the son and heir to King Aegeus.

The strength of Athens lay in its acropolis, the sacred citadel built on the sheer-faced rock that rises above the plain of Attica.

And the seven turns of the labyrinth pattern have frequently been seen as a city's defensive walls. In children's games, running the path can denote an attack on the city. Turf mazes in England are named after Troy, as Troy Town, Troy's Walls or Troy's Hoy. Likewise, in Scandinavia labyrinths are named Trojienborg and Welsh hilltop mazes were once called Caerdroia, 'City of Troy'. Troy was said to have seven walls. Achilles chased

Hector around them before killing him and dragging his body around them again.

Labyrinths near Helsinki go by other city names, such as Ruins of Jerusalem, City of Nineveh and The Walls of Jericho. Joshua attacked the city of Jericho during his conquest of Canaan: God instructed him to circle the city walls once a day for seven days in a row, with seven priests blowing seven trumpets. On the seventh day they were to circle the walls seven times. When Joshua did as God suggested, the walls came tumbling down.

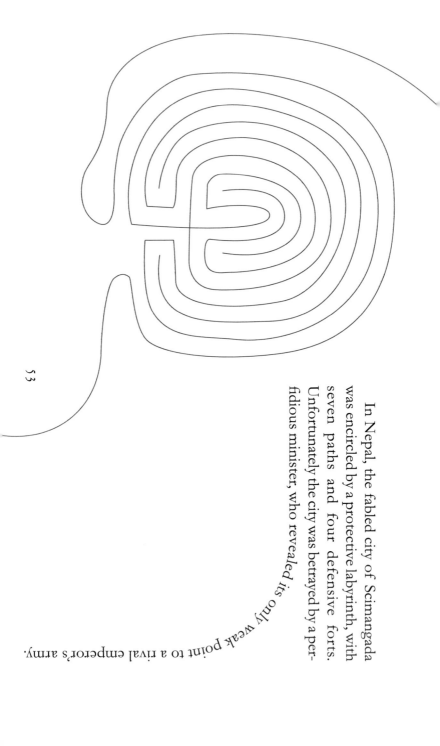

In Nepal, the fabled city of Scimangada was encircled by a protective labyrinth, with seven paths and four defensive forts. Unfortunately the city was betrayed by a perfidious minister, who revealed its only weak point to a rival emperor's army.

Modern cities can be just as labyrinthine as those of legend. In 1993, New College Worcester, a school for blind and visually impaired children, challenged Anneka Rice to build a multisensory maze that replicated features of a modern city: Rice installed pelican crossings, pavements, bollards, scaffolding, postboxes and parked cars. The students were then able to practise negotiating the urban maze in safety.

Victor Hugo has Jean Valjean carry the wounded Marius through the sewer network below Paris in *Les Misérables*:

> The subsoil of Paris, if the eye could penetrate the surface, would present the aspect of a colossal madrepore. A sponge has hardly more defiles and passages than the tuft of earth of fifteen miles' circuit upon which rests the ancient great city. Without speaking of the catacombs, which are a cave apart, without speaking of the inextricable trellis of the gas-pipes, without counting the vast tubular system for the distribution of living water which ends in the hydrants, the sewers of themselves alone form a prodigious dark network under both banks; a labyrinth the descent of which is its clue.

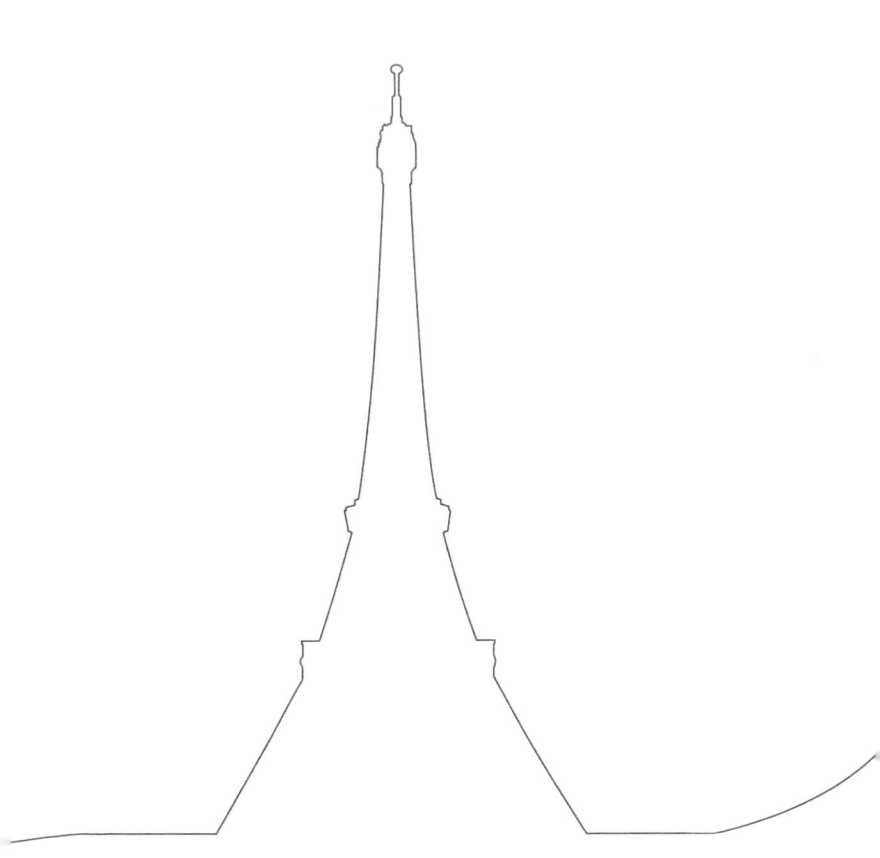

In the next century, Walter Benjamin described another maze below Paris: 'This labyrinth harbours in its interior not one but a dozen blind raging bulls, into whose jaws not one Theban virgin once a year but thousands of anaemic young dressmakers and drowsy clerks every morning must hurl themselves.'

London has a similarly visceral transport system. A permanent artwork called *Labyrinth* was unveiled across the London Underground network recently: artist Mark Wallinger created 270 metal panels, one for every tube station, each displaying a unique labyrinth design. He sees each pattern as a 'mental map, a representation of the orientation and contemplation which are the everyday experience of millions of Londoners and their days spent on the Labyrinthine network'.

Wallinger's labyrinths transform the experience of navigating the city. '*Labyrinth* invites us to juxtapose our experiential London with a mythical realm,' says the author Will Self, 'and to seek within our workaday travels the essence of an odyssey or quest.'

For some the quest inherent in a city is the challenge first to recognize and then to transcend its maze-like qualities. The Situationists believed that Paris's thoroughfares, advertisements, signs and maps were forcing citizens to conform to a capitalist norm. Led by Guy Debord in the 1960s, they championed the concept of the *dérive*: ignoring a city's subliminal routing and drifting instead against the prevailing tides of movement.

Simultaneously, a collective of Parisian writers replicated the Situationists' quest through literary games. Calling themselves OULIPO, short for '*ouvroir de littérature poten-tielle*', 'studio for potential literature', writers such as Raymond Queneau and Georges Perec began constructing artificial constraints for their writing. Perec's 320-page novel *La Disparition*, for example, is a thriller in which a figure called Anton Voyl has disappeared. What's really missing, however, is the letter 'e': Perec wrote the entire novel without using it once.

The British critic Philip Howard, also avoiding the letter 'e', described *La Disparition* as 'a story chock-full of plots and sub-plots, of loops within loops, of trails in pursuit of trails, all of which allow its author an opportunity to display his customary virtuosity as an avant-gardist magi-cian, acrobat and clown'.

Queneau called his fellow Oulipians 'rats' – 'who build the labyrinth from which they try to escape'.

Many animals can be taught to negotiate mazes. Earthworms can remember which way to turn in a maze with one fork, and ants can deal with up to ten. The best maze runners, however, are rats, which have evolved to scurry effortlessly around their extensive underground burrows. Rats can learn mazes quickly and then run them backwards and forwards without a false move.

Early experiments involved placing rats in miniature models of the Hampton Court Maze. Varying the design and difficulty of the maze allows an investigator to study spatial learning and memory in rats' brains, and then to extrapolate general principles to other species, including humans.

In James Dashner's novel *The Maze Runner*, the 'Gladers' are amnesiac boys who discover they are human rats in the centre of an enormous, concrete maze. The mechanical walls are a mile high and each night the design changes. The fastest boys spend the daytime running the maze, attempting to find a way out. It eventually emerges that the Gladers are part of an experiment, designed specifically to test their ability to escape.

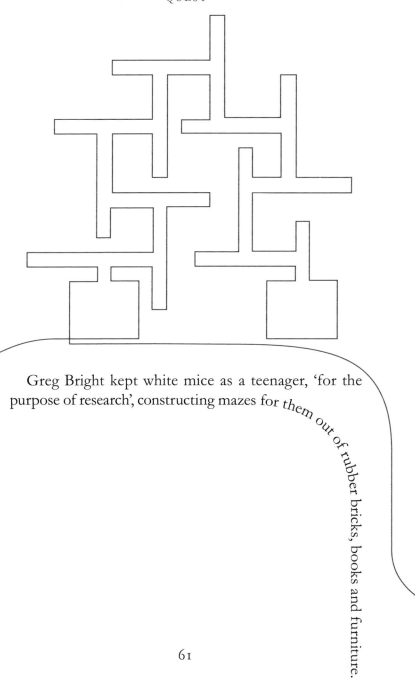

Greg Bright kept white mice as a teenager, 'for the purpose of research', constructing mazes for them out of rubber bricks, books and furniture.

I visited Pilton in 2011, and Michael Eavis showed me the site of Greg's trench maze. All traces of it have since vanished and the area is now a pond fringed with reeds and willows.

I asked Michael what happened after Greg had finished it.

'I got a phone call from Lord Bath,' he told me, 'who was then Lord Weymouth, because he was Lord Bath's son. He said, could he have a look at the maze? So I said, yeah, I mean, pop down.'

Alexander Thynn, now Lord Bath, arrived at Worthy Farm to examine Greg's maze, and asked if he could see it from above.

'I said, well I've got a couple of ladders. We can tie the ladders together with string, and you can go up in the air. [. . .] So we tied these ladders together – it was high as that tree – and up he went, with his funny trousers and leather spat things on his legs. It was hysterical actually. [. . .] Greg and I] held each side of the ladder, and Lord Weymouth, who's actually now Lord Bath [. . .] went on up to the top of that ladder, and it was so dangerous. [. . . He] could have died.'

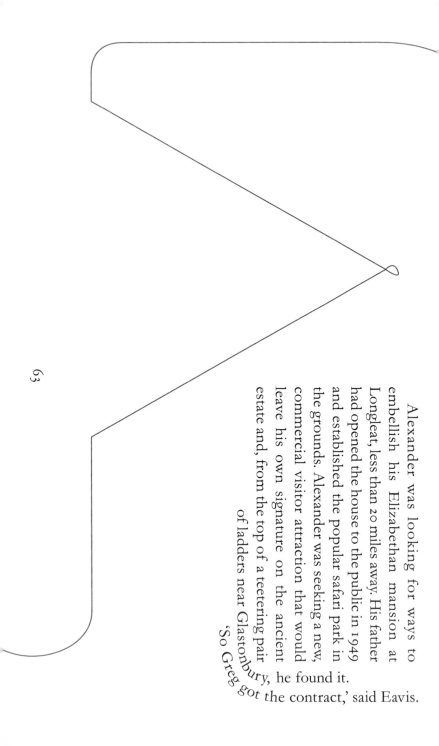

Alexander was looking for ways to embellish his Elizabethan mansion at Longleat, less than 20 miles away. His father had opened the house to the public in 1949 and established the popular safari park in the grounds. Alexander was seeking a new, commercial visitor attraction that would leave his own signature on the ancient estate and, from the top of a teetering pair of ladders near Glastonbury, he found it.

'So Greg got the contract,' said Eavis.

Alexander commissioned Greg to design a maze for Longleat. It must have seemed like an eccentric decision at the time; planting a hedge maze is expensive and there was no certainty that a new maze would be a commercial success.

Initially the plan was to build an L-shaped maze near the front of the house, running down to the lake. There were problems with the site, however, and Greg was offered an alternative space behind the mansion. He was shown a large field and asked how much of it he would like to use, so he drew a line around the entire perimeter and announced that he would fill it with the largest hedge maze in the world.

From the start he knew his maze was going to be fiendish, and this threw up what he called the 'old lady problem': 'You know, when you've got an old lady stuck in it, and you've got to get her out.'

So Longleat actually consists of two mazes. The first is made up of what Greg describes as some 'fairly simple loops'. It's known as the 'frying pan', because you enter along a 'handle' and then you circulate within a contained area until you eventually find a wooden bridge and hop out of the frying pan into the fire. At that point, you have the option to cut your losses and leave through the quick exit; otherwise, you continue into the main body of Greg Bright's spectacular maze.

Longleat surpasses Pilton, not only in size but because it incorporates another principle of maze design: bridges. There are six at Longleat.

Bridges literally add an extra dimension to a maze. In two dimensions, a maze pattern's paths start to limit its complexity: once a proportion of the available space has been filled, the options for filling the remainder are reduced. Bridges relieve this constraint. The maze designer can make links across the maze without connecting the paths in between: he has more control over which sections of the maze are connected, and consequently more opportunities to complicate the design.

Initially, Greg had hoped to include underpasses instead of bridges: moments where one path ducked invisibly beneath another; but in the end this proved too expensive. As it is the hedges cover 1.5 acres and are made up of 16,000 English yew trees, kept trim by a dedicated team of six gardeners, who use stilts to navigate the 1.7 miles of pathways.

The maze opened in 1978 and it was an immediate hit, even though it can take an hour and a half, or even longer, to solve. Since then Lord Bath has added five more mazes to his collection at Longleat, although Greg's original is still the star attraction.

Almost immediately other mazes started to appear, cropping up in amusement parks, city centres and the grounds of stately homes, and a new fellowship of maze designers began to emerge.

Retired British diplomat Randoll Coate designed the Imprint of Man at Lechlade Mill in Gloucestershire, a private maze shaped liked a footprint 'such as would be left by a giant as tall as the Eiffel Tower'. One of its toe-prints is an island built into the mill-stream, accessed by little wooden bridges.

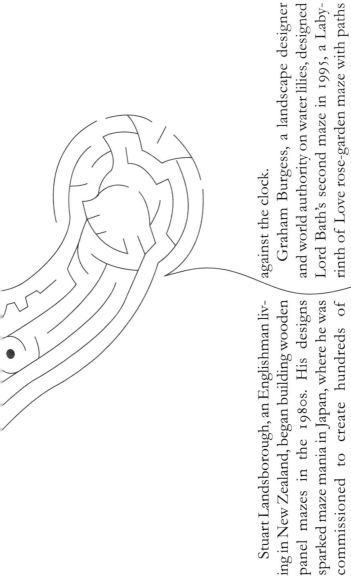

Stuart Landsborough, an Englishman living in New Zealand, began building wooden panel mazes in the 1980s. His designs sparked maze mania in Japan, where he was commissioned to create hundreds of wooden mazes in which teams competed against the clock.

Graham Burgess, a landscape designer and world authority on water lilies, designed Lord Bath's second maze in 1995, a Labyrinth of Love rose-garden maze with paths in the shape of hearts.

Meanwhile, Greg staged a solo exhibition of his maze designs at the Institute of Contemporary Arts in London entitled 'The Maze King: Greg Bright'.

Liberated on paper by the lack of physical constraints, he produced dozens of bewildering designs, accompanied by reassuring comments like 'This maze has no beginning or end', or 'I do not expect you to do this one', or 'Solving the mazes is of little significance'.

The centrepiece of the 1975 exhibition was an enormous, psychedelic 'colour maze', which filled an entire wall. It resembled a vibrant circuit board, with many-hued rectilinear paths worming across it, connecting dozens of differently coloured boxes. It demonstrated Greg's fourth contribution to the principles of maze design, 'conditional movement', meaning that only certain paths are 'available' at any one time. Paths must be approached in the correct way in order to be travelled. In Greg's colour maze, you are only 'allowed' on three different colours at any one time. You collect and discard permissible colours whenever you reach a coloured box.

Four years later, Greg published *Greg Bright's Hole Maze*, in which he used all 48 pages to create one leviathan maze that flows backwards and forwards across the spreads, through myriad holes punched in the paper.

'I saw it being readily deciphered by the first aliens from Outer Space, or by some mutant Newton of the dolphin species?'

In any quest there is a risk of overachieving, and Greg's fascination with the graphic purity of mazes was beginning to make his work less and less accessible.

'If you imagine a big, flat untrammelled area, like a big field or something, and you have a boundary around it – imagine a hedge – you can access anywhere in this field, and it is for that very reason that there are no paths in it. A path is not a matter of access; it is a matter of restriction at the same time. But there is one path, namely the path that the boundary takes. [. . .] If you take this hedge, and you imagine walking inside the hedge, you can imagine a kind of opening out of this – and there's a sense in which one could define a maze as the elaboration of the invagination of a boundary.'

The day of the lottery has arrived.

Every eight years, black Cretan sails appear on the horizon, and slim-waisted soldiers of Minos stride confidently into the Athenian marketplace. The rules of the lottery are well known: tribute must be paid to Crete. Seven young men and seven young women are selected by lot, taken across the sea to the Palace of Minos, and ushered into the Labyrinth. No one returns. The whispers tell of darkness inside, of blood-red walls, a bellowing roar and a pair of glinting horns.

The Cretans sort out the youths of Athens and write their names on potsherds, which are mixed in two great painted bowls. This year, Theseus is amongst them.

The lottery begins.

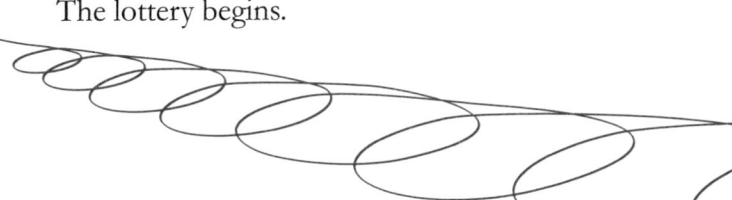

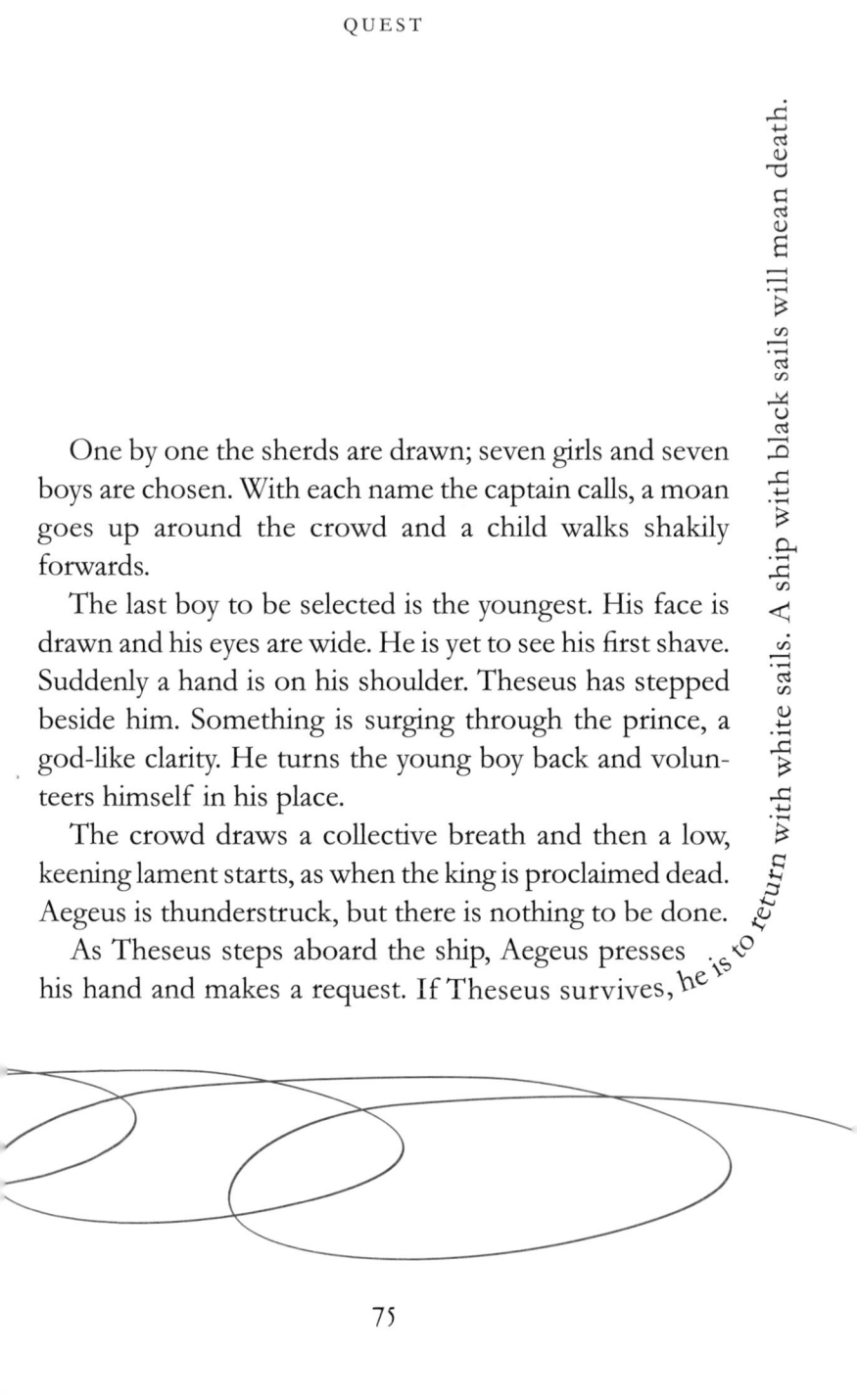

One by one the sherds are drawn; seven girls and seven boys are chosen. With each name the captain calls, a moan goes up around the crowd and a child walks shakily forwards.

The last boy to be selected is the youngest. His face is drawn and his eyes are wide. He is yet to see his first shave. Suddenly a hand is on his shoulder. Theseus has stepped beside him. Something is surging through the prince, a god-like clarity. He turns the young boy back and volunteers himself in his place.

The crowd draws a collective breath and then a low, keening lament starts, as when the king is proclaimed dead. Aegeus is thunderstruck, but there is nothing to be done.

As Theseus steps aboard the ship, Aegeus presses his hand and makes a request. If Theseus survives, he is to return with white sails. A ship with black sails will mean death.

This is a vision of the labyrinth as a web. The poet will never reach the centre, nor will he escape. He is the fly and he is expecting the spider.

Tomb

Labyrinths are the bourn of that undiscovered country from which no traveller returns.

There is a miscellany of eleventh-century alchemical treatises in the Biblioteca Nazionale Marciana in Venice, in which an anonymous fourteenth-century scribe has filled a blank page with a labyrinth and a poem. He encourages readers to see his design 'as the circular path of life', slippery and dangerous, full of twists and turns, like a 'dragon, with his evil wriggling'. Day after day you search for some way out of this terrible prison, as it plays its game with you, until eventually time vanishes and you are received by 'that dark worker, Death'.

The Sanskrit epic *Mahabharata* describes a deadly labyrinth. On the thirteenth day of the Battle of Kurukshetra, the sixteen-year-old warrior Abhimanyu rides out in his chariot. When the Kaurava forces see the single charioteer approaching, they begin to form the *chakra-vyuha* formation, a human labyrinth of warriors, designed to encircle and trap enemies within its coils, but Abhimanyu continues to urge his chariot forwards.

Abhimanyu's mother was Subhadra, sister of Krishna the Supreme Being, and Krishna had made a habit of walking with Subhadra while she was pregnant. On one such walk, Krishna described his battle exploits, explaining at length how to penetrate the seven coils of the *chakra-vyuha*, and he went into such exhaustive military detail that Subhadra soon feel asleep. Inside her womb, however, the unborn Abhimanyu was listening to every word.

Now Abhimanyu storms into the Kaurava defences. Remembering Krishna's words, he negotiates every turn of the *chakra-vyuha* successfully, getting closer and closer to the centre. The Kauravas are amazed at this blazing warrior, carving his way through their ranks.

Unfortunately, all those years ago, Krishna had stopped talking when he realized that Subhadra had fallen asleep, so he never finished explaining how to escape from the *chakra-vyuha*. Abhimanyu reaches the centre of the battle maze, but he can't fight his way out. Trapped, and defending himself valiantly with his own chariot wheel, he is attacked from all sides and eventually falls.

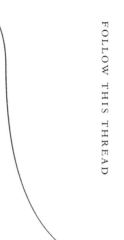

Death frequently lurks at the centre of mazes. A small, tanked pond in the grounds of Blenheim Palace in Oxfordshire is known as 'Rosamond's Well'. It commemorates the sad story of fair Rosamond Clifford, mistress of King Henry II.

To keep his liaisons with Rosamond secret, Henry constructed a 'bower' in the grounds of his palace at Woodstock, now the site of Blenheim.

> *Most peerless was her beauty found,*
> *Her favour and her face;*
> *A sweeter creature in the world,*
> *Could never prince embrace.*

> *Most curiously that bower was built*
> *Of stone and timber strong,*
> *An hundred and fifty doors*
> *Did to this bower belong.*

> *And they so cunningly contriv'd,*
> *With turnings round about,*
> *That none without a clue of thread*
> *Could enter in or out.*

The tale was a favourite amongst Tudor balladeers.

According to the story, Eleanor of Aquitaine, Henry's jealous queen, found the 'clue of thread' and confronted Rosamond at the centre of the bower. She offered Rosamond a choice between a dagger and a cup of poison, while Rosamond pleaded forgiveness.

But nothing could this furious queen
Herewith appeased be,
The cup of deadly poison strong,
Which she held on her knee,

She gave this comely dame to drink,
Who took it from her hand,
And from her bended knees arose,
And on her feet did stand.

When casting up her eyes to heaven,
She did for mercy call,
And drinking up the poison strong
She left her life withal.

The events of Umberto Eco's *The Name of the Rose* take place in an unnamed clifftop abbey west of Pisa. The murder mystery revolves around the maze-like abbey library.

'The library defends itself,' warns the abbot, 'immeasurable as the truth it houses, deceitful as the falsehood it preserves. A spiritual labyrinth, it is also a terrestrial labyrinth. You might enter and you might not emerge.' Guarded by the blind former librarian, Jorge of Burgos, the library contains distorting mirrors, hallucinatory drugs and poisons designed to ward off intruders.

... south tower, where he finds the murderer waiting for him ...

As monks start to die in increasingly gruesome ways, the English Franciscan William of Baskerville races to solve the riddle. He triumphs only after opening a secret door and penetrating to the heart of the maze, the central room of the

Mazes not only contain deadly perils, they can also represent the 'diaphragm', as the novelist Giovanni Mariotti puts it, between the world of the living and the world of the dead. In 1934, the ethnologist Bernard Deacon recorded a pattern traced in the sand on Malekula, an island in the Pacific nation of Vanuatu, over 1,000 miles east of Australia.

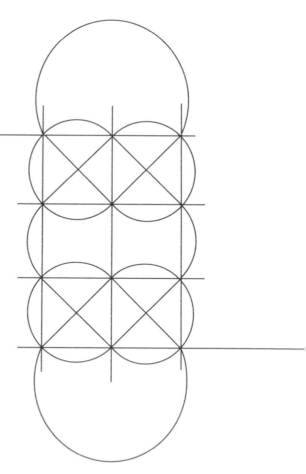

The pattern, known as the *nahal*, matches a design drawn by a fearsome guardian spirit, whom ghosts of the recently deceased meet as they travel along the road to Wies, the Land of the Dead.

The spirit's name is Temes Savsap. She sits beside a large rock in the middle of the sea, guarding the entrance to the afterlife and drawing the *nahal* in the sand. The path along which ghosts must travel runs directly through the middle of the pattern, but as each ghost approaches, Temes rubs out half of the figure and the ghost is forced to stop. The only way to proceed is to remember the design and redraw the missing half, without making a mistake. If you are unable to do so, Temes Savsap loses patience and devours you.

There is a similar maze in North Wales. On the Honey Isle of Anglesey, where the Celtic druids made their final stand against the Romans, there is a Neolithic passage tomb known as Bryn Celli Ddu, 'the mound in the dark grove'. Visitors can still crawl through the burial chamber's narrow entrance, along a tight stone passage, into its earthen interior. Outside stands a 'pattern stone' with labyrinthine lines inscribed on both sides: sinuous grooves that form spirals and dead ends as you trace them with your finger.

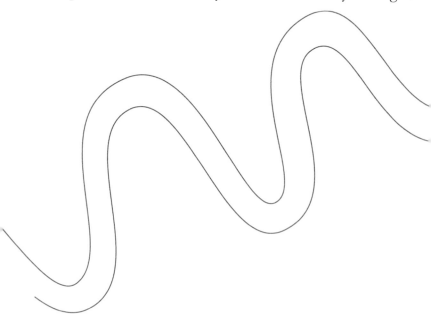

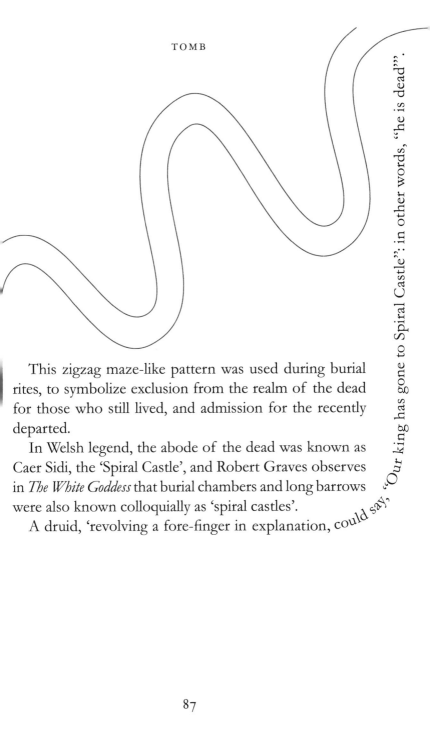

This zigzag maze-like pattern was used during burial rites, to symbolize exclusion from the realm of the dead for those who still lived, and admission for the recently departed.

In Welsh legend, the abode of the dead was known as Caer Sidi, the 'Spiral Castle', and Robert Graves observes in *The White Goddess* that burial chambers and long barrows were also known colloquially as 'spiral castles'.

A druid, 'revolving a fore-finger in explanation, could say, "Our king has gone to Spiral Castle": in other words, "he is dead"'.

The comparison with death may explain why mazes have also been used to commemorate the departed. Herodotus visited an enormous Egyptian sepulchre in the fifth century BCE, known as 'the Labyrinth'. It was built on the north shore of Lake Moeris, near Crocodilopolis, the City of Crocodiles.

'The Labyrinth surpasses even the pyramids,' he wrote: 'it has twelve courts covered in, with gates facing one another, six upon the North side and six upon the South, joining on one to another, and the same wall surrounds them all outside.'

Herodotus was permitted to explore the upper chambers, and 'the goings this way and that way through the courts, which were admirably adorned, afforded endless matter for marvel', but the chambers below ground were out of bounds, because they contained the tombs of holy crocodiles.

In 1888, the Egyptologist Flinders Petrie identified the site. Amongst the debris he unearthed the granite tomb effigy of Amenemhat III, the twelfth-dynasty pharaoh who commissioned the Labyrinth complex as his own mausoleum.

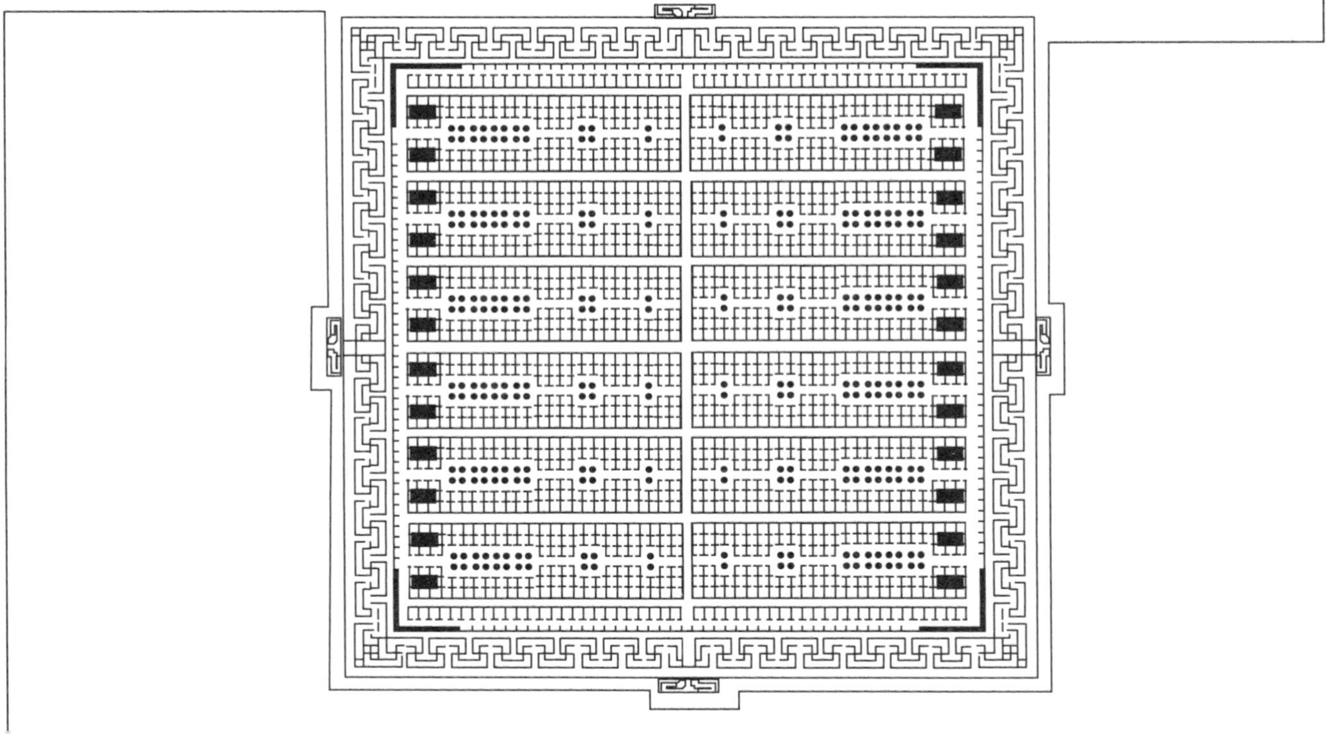

On the grounds of Los Alamos, an estate in western Argentina, amidst the poplar trees that sweep up the Andes, Jorge Luis Borges's name is marked out by 12,000 English boxwood shrubs. This memorial maze, El Laberinto de Borges, was designed by the writer's friend Randoll Coate. It resembles an open book and conceals images from Borges's life and work, including a walking stick, an hourglass, a question mark and a tiger's face. El Laberinto de Borges has recently been recreated in Venice, in the grounds of the Abbey of San Giorgio Maggiore. The Venetian maze has been fitted with a handrail for the blind and partially sighted, along which Borges's story 'The Garden of Forking Paths' has been translated into Braille.

In this story, a vast book is revealed to be a labyrinth, containing every possible version of the future in a 'growing, dizzying net of divergent, convergent and parallel times'.

In some futures the story's protagonists die. In others they don't.

'At one time, perhaps I felt a certain commitment towards them, but not now,' Greg Bright wrote in 1973. 'Now, and for some time, I have ceased even to like mazes. I dislike them.'

'The love-affair is over,' he reiterated in 1975; 'I have opened their secrets. Now, I am pimping for them.'

Finally, in 1979, he admitted: 'Since digging the Pilton Maze in 1971, I have been trying to abandon mazes. [. . .] I began to be drawn back to mazes because of "the thrill of being lost" and "the strangeness of routing" and their "mystery" – an aspect that now particularly disgusts me.'

In an interview with the *Kentucky Daily News*, Bright described his dream of the ultimate maze:

> 'The walls are 12 feet tall, so the person in the maze can't see out. When he enters the maze the door behind him locks, and the attendants go away. [. . .] No place to eat, no place to drink. It's a matter of solving the maze or not surviving.'

'His eyes glitter as he describes this,' the interviewer writes. 'One senses he would welcome the chance to tackle this life-or-death challenge himself.'

In 1979, Bright disappeared.

He published no more maze books and never built another maze.

Centre

Theseus is washed and oiled and prepared for the games.

Funeral games are held every tribute time, in memory of Minos's dead son, but Athenians never usually compete. This year, Theseus has volunteered.

The crowd cheers as the athletes step into the field. Men shout and exchange wagers; women shriek with laughter and cover their eyes.

Most of the events are familiar, and Theseus excels at them all. There is the *stade*, the sprint; the *dolichos*, the long-distance run; the *pale*, wrestling; and the *pankration*, free fighting. But the most prestigious Cretan event is new to him: *taurokathapsia*, bull-leaping.

One by one, massive bulls are loosed into the stadium, and contestants run at them, grab them by the horns and vault over their heads, springing lightly off their backs in an elegant somersault. It is an aesthetic contest, but it requires absolute courage and perfect timing.

Minos and Pasiphae watch the games from gilded thrones. Below them, their daughter, the priestess Ariadne, watches Theseus as he jumps. Elsewhere in the crowd, Daedalus is also observing, impressed by his fellow countryman.

Later, glistening and crowned with laurels, Theseus steps up to salute King Minos, and finds himself facing Ariadne.

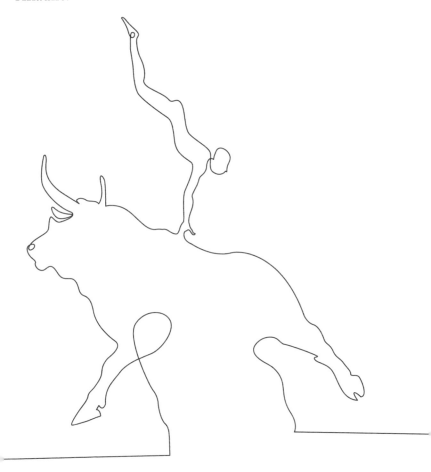

Now the women enter the field. They are dressed in fine linen, which billows about them as they walk, and their ringlets shimmer down their backs. Theseus finds a space in the stands amongst his companions.

A dancing floor is inlaid in the ground, a flat pattern marked in smooth black and white marble. The priestesses acknowledge Minos and Pasiphae, and then, holding each other lightly by the wrists, they begin to dance. Led by Ariadne, the line of dancers curves and turns and flows back, following the coils of the pattern, as the women bend and sway and whirl around the floor.

The crowd is rapt. Theseus cannot tear his eyes away from Ariadne. The priestesses describe the coils of the Labyrinth, every delicate turn of their feet representing a tortuous knot of the passageways he will soon be facing, but at this moment he is consumed by her dancing figure, her face, the flash of her eye each time she looks his way.

That night, she visits him. He wakes with a finger across his lips.

'Your name, Athenian?' she whispers.

'Theseus.'

'Tomorrow night you face the Labyrinth.'

He looks at her, bovine.

'I have spoken with Daedalus and he has revealed to me its secret. Quickly, I shall tell you.'

He touches her arm.

'How can I thank you?'

'When you and your companions escape, take me with you.'

She questions him with an imperious look, still the priestess. He nods simply and she bends low to whisper in his ear. She describes her half-brother, the Minotaur.

A monstrous bull appeared in the land of Uruk, in the twenty-seventh century BCE. Forests of trees withered as it passed; fields of grain crumbled to ash. When it drank from the Euphrates, the water sank by seven cubits; when it snorted, the blast drove fissures into the earth, engulfing hundreds of people. This awesome bull was Gugalanna, the Bull of Heaven, led down from his starry enclosure by Ishtar, the Mesopotamian goddess of sex and violence.

The *Epic of Gilgamesh* tells how King Gilgamesh, shepherd of Uruk-the-Sheepfold, spurned Ishtar's amorous advances, and how she, spitting with rage, implored her father, Anu, to release Gugalanna to kill the king. If he didn't, she threatened, she would smash open the gates of the Underworld and raise hordes of zombie dead to devour the living.

Gilgamesh was tall and proud. Before the walls of Uruk, he and his companion Enkidu faced the Bull of Heaven. Enkidu grabbed it by the tail, while Gilgamesh seized the horns and, with a butcher's skill, drove his knife deep into the slaughter-spot, slaying the celestial beast.

'Most likely the Greek fable of the Minotaur is a late and clumsy version of far older myths,' wrote Borges, in *The Book of Imaginary Beings*, 'the shadow of other dreams still more full of horror.'

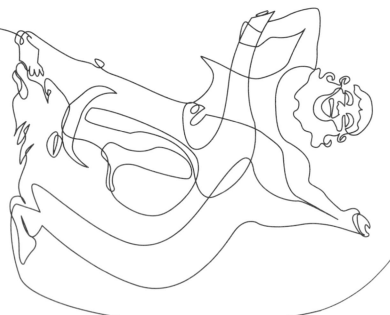

For the Mesopotamians, Gugalanna, our Taurus, was the first sign of the zodiac, marking the sun's ecliptic position at the vernal equinox, the birth of each new year. The episode from the *Epic of Gilgamesh* represents a ritual sacrifice, a cosmic drama in which the sun god Gilgamesh vanquishes the old year's winter and ushers in a new spring.

'[S]tripped of his mythical features,' writes James Frazer in *The Golden Bough*, the Minotaur 'was nothing but a bronze image of the sun represented as a man with a bull's head.'

Frazer identifies the story of Theseus and the Minotaur with the cyclical renewal of Minos's power. Every eight years, so the legend goes, Minos renewed his sacred kingship. He would travel to Mount Ida, Crete's highest mountain, to commune with Zeus in the sacred cave where the god was born.

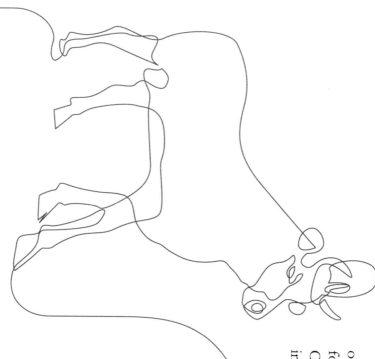

The Athenian tribute coincided with this octennial cycle, and Frazer imagines that foreign youths would have been brought to Crete at this time to be offered to a brazen image of the bull-headed sun god.

'In order to renew the solar fires, human victims may have been sacrificed to the idol by being roasted in its hollow body,' he writes, 'or placed on its sloping hands and allowed to roll into a pit of fire.

[. . .]

'[I]t would seem to follow that the sinuous lines of the labyrinth which the dancers followed in their evolutions may have represented the ecliptic, the sun's apparent annual path in the sky.'

The crowd is now silent.

In the clear ground before the entrance to the Labyrinth, the band of Athenians huddles together, holding hands, tripping over breathless prayers. By torchlight, Minos stands in the robes of a hierophant, intoning the rites, splashing skins of blood-dark wine over a two-horned altar stone, blessing the human offering. Behind him, the door to the Labyrinth stands open. A single taper flares in the entrance.

Minos steps aside and soldiers push the Athenians forwards with spears. The crowd breathes together. Theseus steps out and leads the way, his courage a lifeline to the others. Proudly they walk towards the entrance. Theseus turns his head a fraction and catches Ariadne's eye. She is unbreathing, eyes glistening.

Then he has stepped into the Labyrinth and his companions file in behind him. The door swings shut behind them and they hear the thick bar thudding into the brackets. There is no way back.

The shadowy walls constrict with sudden claustrophobia: beyond a few yards of illumin-

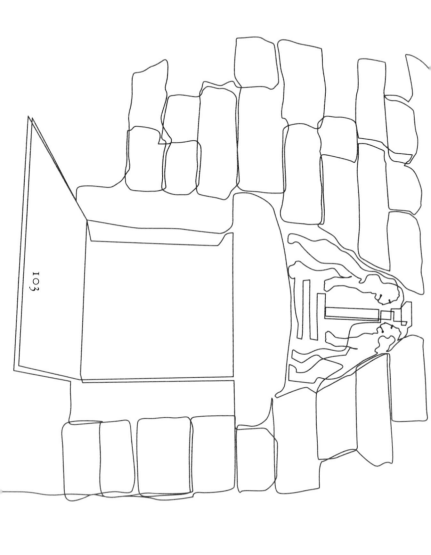

103

sageway, there is nothing but darkness.

Theseus pulls the taper from the wall and leads the group forwards. The passage curves and slopes downwards. They enter a circular, domed cavern, from which seven doorways lead into darkness. The torch sends monstrous shadows chasing around the walls.

Theseus explains what Ariadne has told him. He will go alone into the depths of the Labyrinth, he will slay the Minotaur and he will return. He produces her gift: a large ball of fine, scarlet thread.

He ties one end to a ring in the wall. Dumbly the Athenians watch as he places the ball of thread in the centre of the cavern and spins it like a top. Its gyrations slow and grow eccentric, until, drawn by the imperceptible slope of the cavern floor, it unravels towards one of the seven doorways. Rolling silently out of sight, there is now a clear scarlet thread for Theseus to follow.

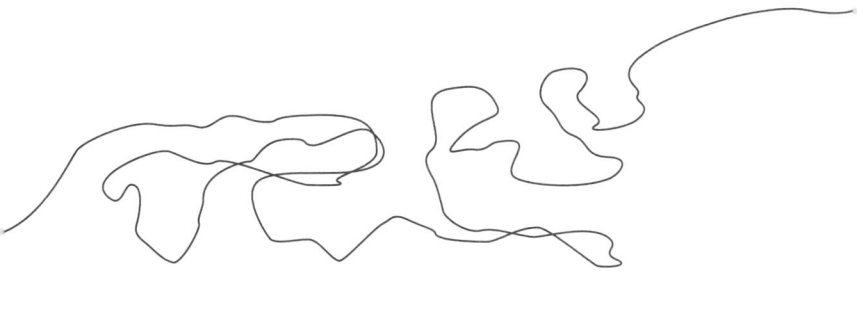

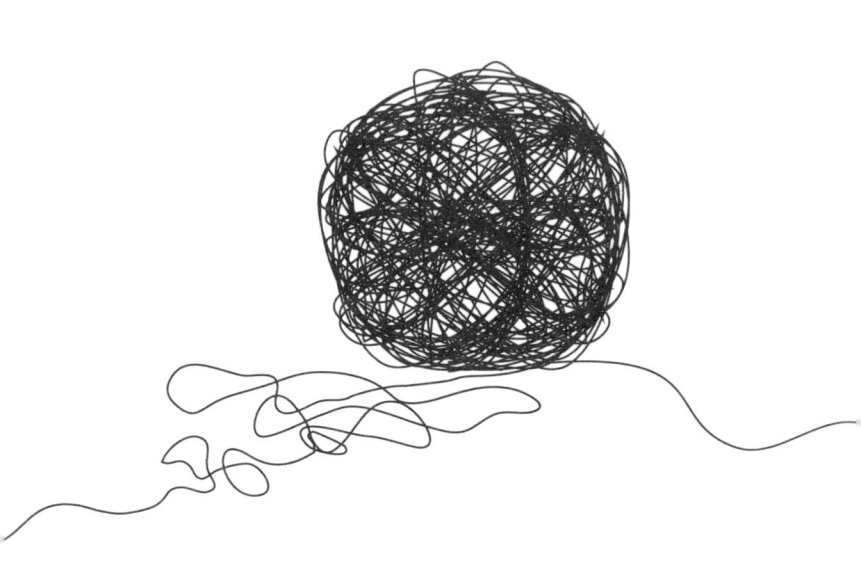

Theseus shouts with triumph, and that is when they hear it, far off and baffled by myriad intervening passages: unmistakably the roar of a gigantic bull.

Theseus looks into his companions' faces. Then, holding the flaming torch ahead of him, he sets off into the Labyrinth.

'*Semibovemque virum, semivirumque bovem*', wrote Ovid, 'man, half-bull, bull, half-man'.

The Minotaur has a man's body, with a man's hands and arms, but on his muscular shoulders he carries the head of a bull, with a snorting, slavering muzzle, wide-set eyes and wicked horns. He sees obliquely from his wedge-shaped skull, which he jerks from side to side to glare sidelong at whatever's in front of him.

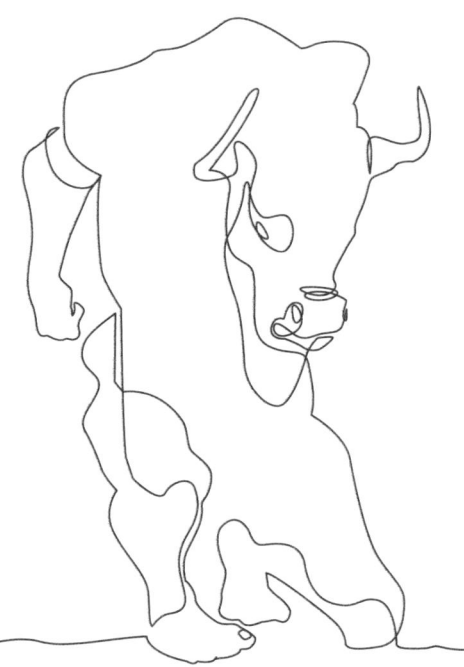

He is composite, physically and mentally. He has both a bull's instincts and the vestiges of human intellect, and the combination is his only weakness: his bestiality obscures his reason and his intelligence confounds his reflexes.

In 1931, Picasso illustrated Ovid's *Metamorphoses* and the cover for the magazine *Minotaure*. The Minotaur recurs throughout Picasso's work of the period: his monster carouses with louche artists, snores behind floral curtains, makes ferocious love to beautiful women and dies in arenas surrounded by impassive faces. For Picasso, the Minotaur was the exuberant, animal aspect of human nature but also the aspiring aesthete, trapped inside an uncivilized body.

Man Ray photographed Picasso in 1934, the same year he created 'Minotaur', a photograph of a naked female torso resembling a ghostly bull's skull, with arms raised, her head, hands and stomach lost in shadow.

A photograph of Picasso appeared in *Life* magazine fifteen years later: the picture shows a topless, portly man in white shorts standing on a beach, with his face obscured by a papier-mâché bull's head.

'If all the ways I have been along were marked on a map and joined with a line, wrote Picasso to his friend, Romuald Dor de la Souchère, it might represent a Minotaur.'

Theseus follows the thread, deeper and deeper, down staircases, along galleries, through doorway after doorway, the torchlight flaring shadows around him and playing tricks with his mind's eye.

The Minotaur must be close now. The walls are dark with blood. Somewhere nearby he catches cattle sounds, the clink of horn against stone. He glances over his shoulder. He imagines breath on the back of his neck. His skin prickles. The animal reek is thickening the air. It curdles in his nose and mouth. He wipes his dripping forehead.

It must have smelt him by now. Theseus thinks himself into the Minotaur's head, listening to his own footsteps approaching, the soft pad of an intruder's leather sandals on the familiar stones, maddening self-assurance.

The thread runs out.

Bellowing, the Minotaur rushes forwards, towards the trespasser in his Labyrinth.

Borges imagines the Minotaur's point of view.

He wanders stone galleries, playing solitary games of hide and seek, charging till he feels dizzy. He plays his favourite game with an imaginary friend he calls the 'other Asterion'. Together they wander the Labyrinth, laughing.

Every few years, a group of young people enter his house, and he runs to them joyfully, dispatching them in a few minutes. He finds their lifeless bodies helpful for distinguishing one room from another.

Borges said he owed his story, 'The House of Asterion', to a painting by G. F. Watts, which is now in the Tate Collection in London. Watts intended 'to hold up to detestation the bestial and brutal', but his Minotaur shows a pitiable, sympathetic creature gazing out to sea, absent-mindedly crushing a songbird in his fist.

Asterion longs for the arrival of his 'redeemer', someone who will lead him to a place with fewer rooms and fewer doors. He wonders what this redeemer will be like, a bull or a man, or perhaps a bull with the face of a man.

When he finally meets Theseus, the Minotaur scarcely defends himself. He is surprised, perhaps, at how closely the other Asterion resembles his own reflection.

When we were come to where the thigh revolves
Exactly on the thickness of the haunch,
The Guide, with labour and with hard-drawn breath,

Turned round his head where he had had his legs,
And grappled to the hair, as one who mounts,
So that to Hell I thought we were returning.

The Minotaur wakes up in a labyrinth of glass, a maze of mirrors, 'crouching face to face with its reflection, but also with the reflections of its reflections'.

In Friedrich Dürrenmatt's story 'Minotaurus', the Minotaur loves its new labyrinth. Yelping, it cavorts through the maze, dancing 'like a monstrous child', 'like a monstrous father of itself', 'like a monstrous god through the universe of its reflections'. When human creatures start to appear, he dances with them too, until they stop moving.

But one day he starts to doubt.

'He retreated. So did his reflection. And gradually it dawned on him that he was facing himself. He tried to flee, but wherever he turned, he always stood facing himself, he was walled in by himself, everywhere he himself was mirrored by the labyrinth, on and on without end.'

Eventually another Minotaur appears and the Minotaur howls for joy at no longer being the only one, but when they dance, the new Minotaur sinks a dagger deep into the fleshy hump at the back of his neck, and the murdered beast slumps to the ground.

Lifting off his bull's-head mask, Theseus disappears silently from the hall of black mirrors.

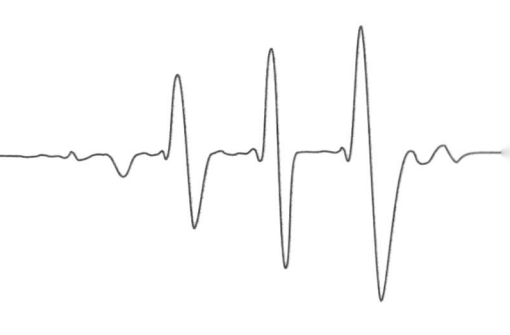

At the age of about six months, so the psychoanalyst Jacques Lacan believed, an infant recognizes its own figure in the looking glass. At that age, a child does not have coordinated control of its whole body, so it feels a disconcerting contrast between the image in the mirror, which looks cohesive and complete, and its own disjointed internal experience. This tension provokes a feeling of aggression towards the seemingly superior mirror-baby.

As infants we resolve this mental fight by making a cognitive leap: we learn to identify with the mirror image, seeing it not as a rival but as our own self, and this revelation is accompanied by a sense of jubilation: in one perceptive breakthrough we have both dispatched an imaginary enemy and gained a newfound sense of ourselves as a coherent human being.

Meeting a doppelgänger as an adult, however, unsettles that conviction. It externalizes our reflection and reinstates the old confrontation. It suggests a parallel life, paths untaken. It questions, as Freud put it, 'all the suppressed acts of volition that fostered the illusion of Free Will'. We see ourselves objectively, straitjacketed by the identity we have constructed through our choices.

Francisco Scaramanga, circus performer turned world-class
assassin, stands back-to-back with James Bond on a beach
in Thailand. They have been circling each other throughout
The Man with the Golden Gun, and finally they meet for a duel.
After 20 paces, Bond turns and shoots, but Scaramanga
has disappeared into an underground cave system, which

turns out to be a private funhouse.

Bond creeps warily through a mechanized hall of mirrors, surrounded by his own shifting reflection, meeting invisible panes of glass and sheer drops. Nick Nack, Scaramanga's accomplice, laughs from an omniscient control room where he monitors proceedings, orchestrating light and sound effects, his disembodied voice ringing through the maze.

In order to defeat his enemy, Bond must become his own doppelgänger. He disappears from Nick Nack's screens, and Scaramanga is lured out into the open, at which point Bond's waxwork dummy swivels and shoots him: Bond has switched positions with his own mannequin.

'Where is he?' gasps Britt Ekland, running up to Roger Moore.

'Flat on his *coup de grâce*.'

Mirror mazes were invented in the late nineteenth century. They consist of multiple mirrors, angled cleverly to create the illusion of size and distance. In Switzerland, for example, at the Glacier Garden in Lucerne, a small mirror maze from 1896 features fountains, Moorish colonnades, flower gardens, faux vistas and a flock of peacocks. Unlike a hedge maze, which confuses by throwing up barriers, a mirror maze presents the equally disorienting illusion of limitless freedom.

In the fifteenth century, Leonardo da Vinci imagined a minimum mirror maze. He drew a sketch of a man surrounded by eight reflective surfaces. Below it he wrote, in mirror-writing: 'If you make eight flat surfaces, each two ells wide and three ells high, and arrange them in a circular fashion such that they form an octagon [. . .] then a man standing inside it can see himself infinitely from all sides.'

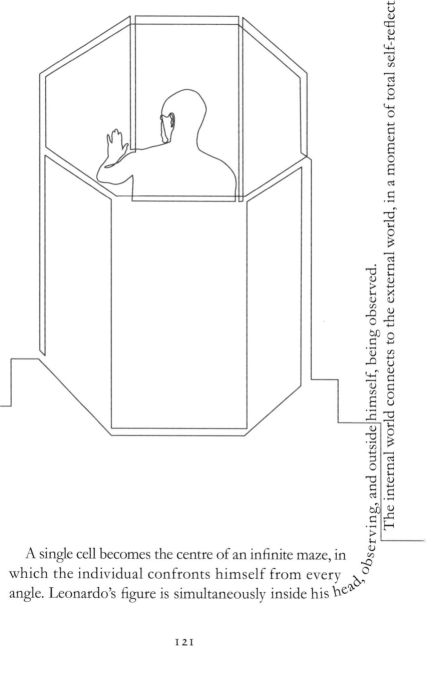

A single cell becomes the centre of an infinite maze, in which the individual confronts himself from every angle. Leonardo's figure is simultaneously inside his head, observing, and outside himself, being observed. The internal world connects to the external world, in a moment of total self-reflection.

Theseus's encounter with the Minotaur is known as the 'Minotauromachy'. It is a wrestling match and a moment of revelation, but the details are mysterious.

In Picasso's etching of that title, a giant Minotaur confronts an unflinching girl carrying a candle, while a bearded man escapes up a ladder and a wounded female bullfighter collapses across a snarling horse.

In Harrison Birtwhistle's opera *The Minotaur*, it is the moment the Minotaur finally acquires human speech, a faculty he has previously experienced only in dreams.

In *The Minotaur Takes a Cigarette Break*, Theseus 'barters for his life'.

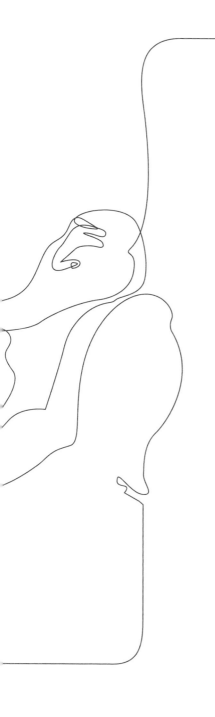

'In the Labyrinth all deals are shady. Skull-duggery holds sway. From the front door ashen Theseus puts on a good face, touts his victory [...] while from the back the Minotaur skulks into a tepid eternity.' Steven Sherrill's novel introduces the Minotaur sitting on an empty pickle bucket in the year 2000. 'M' lives in North Carolina, flipping patties at Grub's Rib roadside diner. Five thousand years earlier, he and Theseus shook hands at the centre of the Labyrinth and agreed not to fight. Theseus could claim he killed a monster, while the Minotaur slipped away, exchanging infamy for freedom.

The historian of religion, Mircea Eliade, argues that many of the episodes in the myth of Theseus are garbled descriptions of ancient initiatory rituals. He describes the Ganda tradition of Central Africa, once practised in the Kuba Kingdom between the tributaries of the Congo River: a man would disappear into a dark cave, while a group of novices gathered around the entrance. Deep inside the tunnel, the man would shout and rattle sticks, and the novices were told he was battling violent spirits. The man then daubed his body with goat's blood, staggered out of the cave and collapsed. The king then ordered the terrified novices to enter the cave one by one.

They thought they were facing a monster; in truth they met nothing more than the limits of their own fear.

'A maze requires no Minotaur,' wrote Umberto Eco; 'it is its own Minotaur.'

'A walker leaving a labyrinth is not the same person who entered it,' writes Hermann Kern in his monumental book, *Through the Labyrinth*, 'but has been born again into a new phase or level of existence; the centre is where death and rebirth occur.'

He descended into Hell;
The third day, he rose again from the dead.

In the Christian tradition of the Harrowing of Hell, described in the Apostles' Creed, Jesus descends into Hell after he was crucified, and wrestles with the Devil, before raising the virtuous dead and leading them in a parade up to Heaven.

To escape the maze at Leeds Castle, in Kent, you must similarly pass through the Underworld.

Descending from the central raised mound, you continue down through a disguised entrance, spiralling into an underground shellhouse grotto, in which a grotesque giant's face spews water into a fountain. A sinuous subterranean passage leads you past a driftwood sculpture of a horned beast before you emerge again into the sunlight.

At the heart of the maze, the hero meets a reflection of himself; the turn at the centre is the triumph of life over death.

In the *Mahabharata*, the sage Kaca is swallowed by the demon Shukra. When he is regurgitated, he has learned the secret of immortality.

Theseus gropes his way back through the darkness, his torch extinguished, winding his thread back into a ball.

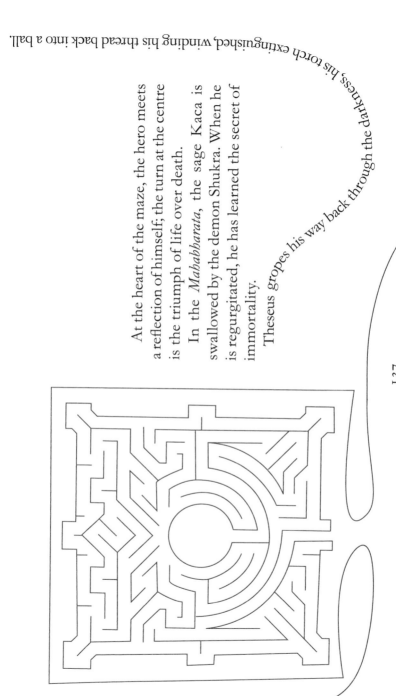

'One ideal is to have consciousness without identity – certainly, I could fancy it.

'But of course it's an asymptote. It's impossible to reach consciousness without identity – but it's an attractive proposition.

'When you get to the centre of a maze [...] you've found the centre, you've found yourself, the self that you wanted to have lost – it's a complete contradiction.

'There you are, dead centre, and I think there's a sense in which it does map on to death.

'With death, you've disburdened yourself [. . .] you're freed from all this stuff, but at the same time, at the price of having no more freedom. That's the contradiction of gain and loss of absolute freedom in death.

'In the centre of Longleat, I wanted to inflect this dead position of the centre, so I built a little tower – well, I didn't do it with my own hands, but I instructed one to be built – so that you can then see over the whole maze.

'And this reflective position inflects death back into life in some way, I think.'

'or maybe he got lost in one of his mazes, who knows?'

That summer I was driving around the UK visiting mazes. As I learned more about Greg, I became fascinated by his story and increasingly curious to find out what happened to him after 1979.

'Nobody knows where he went,' Jeff said. 'Maybe he changed his name,

I set out to look for Greg Bright.

I contacted Jeff Saward, the world's leading maze historian and editor of *Caerdroia*, the journal for the study of mazes and labyrinths. If anyone knew of Greg's whereabouts, I thought, it would be him. We met at the inaugural Saffron Walden Maze Festival in 2011.

'Greg Bright is a very mysterious person,' Jeff told me. '[He] basically disappeared off the face of the planet. There were rumours that he'd emigrated to Australia, and various attempts to track him down, including by his publishers. They contacted me some years ago asking me if I knew where he was. [. . .] They never did find him as far as I know.'

Womb

'Except seven, none returned from Caer Sidi.'

One of the oldest poems in Welsh, the cryptic 'Spoils of Annwfn', describes Caer Sidi, the realm of the dead, as royal, gloomy, four-cornered and high, with steep, shelving sides. It is ruled by the White Goddess, Arianrhod, and located at the back of the North Wind. Its position is marked in the sky by the constellation Corona Borealis.

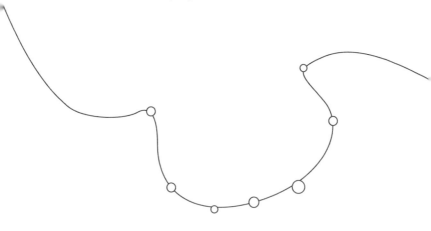

The dead are usually forbidden to leave Caer Sidi, but 'The Spoils of Annwfn' tells how seven heroes have made the miraculous journey home.

We can guess at who they might have been. Robert Graves speculates that 'among those eligible for the honour were Theseus, Hercules, Amathaon, Arthur, Gwydion, Harpocrates, Kay, Owain, Daedalus, Orpheus and Cuchulain'.

Theseus emerges from the deadly Labyrinth, but only with the assistance of Ariadne.

Graves points out that the Welsh form of Ariadne is Arianrhod, the White Goddess.

The Athenian youths hear a creature stumbling
and thudding towards them, bumping the
passage walls as it approaches, emerging
from the shadowy depths of the Labyrinth.

They feel for each other's hands.

Suddenly Theseus bursts into the domed
chamber, reeking with dark blood, reeling in
the umbilical thread, gasping for fresh air.

He greets his companions and they
hurry up the sloping passage. Ariadne is
waiting for them.

Knossos is silent and dark. Two guards
slump lifeless against the wall. Ariadne and
Theseus share a glance: their way is clear
and the Labyrinth is empty.

She grasps his hand and they run towards
the harbour. From a high window, Daedalus watches the group flit through the
winding streets, Ariadne picking the surest
and fastest route between the slumbering
houses.

They choose the same slim barque on
which they sailed from Athens and Theseus gives the order to stave in the hulls of
the other ships. In the city, they hear the
alarm sound.

Hastily, they jump aboard. As Minos's
carriage draws up to the port wall, their
ship gathers speed out of the harbour
mouth and into the dark seas beyond.

When *The Maze Maker* was published in New York, a man came up to Michael Ayrton and said, 'I've read your book. I want one.'

The man was Armand Erpf, a Wall Street stockbroker, and he commissioned Ayrton to design a maze for his country estate at Arkville, amidst the Catskill Mountains, Upstate New York.

Ayrton's Arkville Maze was unveiled in 1969, the largest masonry maze since antiquity. He selected a position with a natural declivity, so that although the top of the maze appears level, the paths gradually descend and the walls get higher and higher as you approach the centre. The maze has two goals, in fact: one plastered with red stucco, in which Ayrton's sculpture of the Minotaur hunches with clenched fists; and one panelled with bronze mirrors, with a sculpture of Daedalus working and Icarus launching into the sky.

Erpf saw humans as naturally curved creatures, so he commissioned a maze made entirely of smooth organic curves. Ayrton drew inspiration from the coils of the guts and the wrinkles of the brain, and particularly the shape of the womb.

The way in and the way out of Ayrton's maze is the birth channel. The mystery of conception takes place at the centre.

'[T]he winding paths are the intestines,' wrote Freud, 'Ariadne's thread, the umbilical cord.'

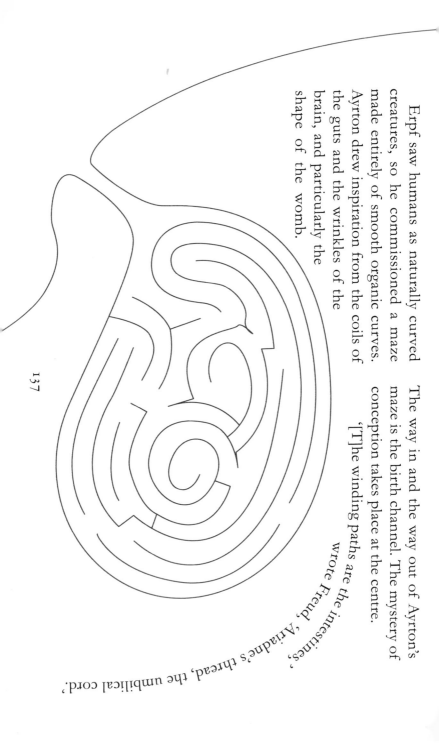

'Rub saffron with water from the Ganges and use it to draw the *chakra-vyuh* on a bronze plate, rinse it off with water from the Ganges, then give it to the labouring mother to drink, and birth will shortly ensue and the pains of labour will be eased.'

This piece of advice for expectant mothers is found in a modern book of Indian rituals, the *Vrhad Karmakanda Baddhati*.

Magical tantric labyrinths have been used to ease the pains of labour in north-western India for more than 400 years. The labyrinth represents the mother's uterus, and swallowing the pattern helps the child navigate the tortuous journey from the womb to the outside world. The designs are known as Abhyumani Yantra, 'tools of Abhimanyu'.

In the physiognomy of ducks, this metaphor has evolved more literally. Rape is so engrained in anatine culture that female mallards have developed corkscrew-shaped vaginas with as many as eight cul-de-sacs, to prevent fertilization from unwelcome sperm. As a result, all nascent duck eggs must navigate the convoluted channel in reverse.

For the Hopi tribe of northern Arizona, the labyrinth is the sacred symbol known as Tápu'at, the 'Mother and Child'.

It represents a concept in Hopi mythology known as the Emergence, spiritual rebirth from one world to another: from the Third World of Kuskurza, for example, to the Fourth World of Túwaqachi, in which we live today.

'[T]he straight line emerging from the entrance is not connected with the maze,' explains Frank Waters in *Book of the Hopi*. 'Its two ends symbolize the two stages of life – the unborn child within the womb of Mother Earth and the child after it is born, the line symbolizing the umbilical cord and the path of the Emergence. [. . .] The inside lines represent the foetal membranes which enfold the child within the womb, and the outside lines the mother's arms which hold it later.'

The symbol is common to other Native American tribes in North and Central America. The Pima of southern Arizona call it the house of I'itoi, the mischievous creator god. The Guna of Panama call the cross at the centre of the labyrinth the Tree of Life, through which the Earth Mother gives birth to her children.

In 1979, the same year that Greg Bright vanished at the age of 28, another 28-year-old maze maker appeared on the scene.

Adrian Fisher, a management consultant, had designed a holly maze in his parents' garden at Throop, near Bournemouth. He was introduced to Randoll Coate, 70 years old by this time, and together they founded Minotaur Designs, the world's first professional firm of maze designers.

Minotaur Designs specialized in 'symbolic' mazes, in which the patterns of paths form pictures when viewed from above.

The Marlborough Maze at Blenheim Palace, for example, is the world's largest symbolic maze: it commemorates the first duke's victory at the Battle of Blenheim, with cannon, banners and trumpets.

Coate left the partnership in 1986, the same year that Borges died, and Fisher renamed the company after himself, Adrian Fisher Mazes Ltd. He has since been responsible for over 700 mazes in 35 different countries.

He has designed hedge mazes, mirror mazes, water mazes, brick mazes, mosaic mazes and colour mazes, and he pioneered the seasonal maize mazes that now fill cornfields every summer. He has worked mazes into municipal pavements, national tourist promotions and Dubai skyscrapers.

Where Bright was fascinated by the 'signification of raw line', Fisher is interested in visitor experiences.

'We want to create settings where families can grow,' he told me, when I visited him at his home in Dorset. 'Young men and young women marry, start a family, bring up their children, want to do things together. [. .] It's great fun to create settings where these bits of family growth can happen.'

He led me around the display maze in his garden, asking me to imagine moveable sections and hidden lasers.

'I go along here and I break an electronic beam but I don't realize it, and then I break another electronic beam and don't realize it, and then this row of fountains jumps up and blocks my path, because this is the maze that thinks,' he said.

'And I wait for the water to drop, but it's not going to. And so I think, fair enough. So I come backwards and I break this beam, and then I break the first beam, at which point the maze says, "Ah, you see! You give in? You give in? Fine!" The water drops. Now you can come through. Just so we know who's running the place.'

Fisher has installed this kind of interactive gadgetry in mazes at Edinburgh Zoo and Legoland Windsor.

The only way to escape his private maze is to admit defeat. 'All you can do is say, "I give in to Fisher."' He plans to build a spring-loaded wooden seat, on which you collapse in despair. Your weight releases a catch, the seat slides back and the maze's goal is revealed.

'Great fun!'

zes are transformative spaces. At the end of his animated film of *Alice's Adventures in Wonderland*, Walt Disney included a climactic maze sequence, and at Disneyland Paris there is a hedge maze called Alice's Curious Labyrinth.

Alice's journeys through Wonderland and Looking-Glass Country are entirely maze-like: confusing, circular and frustrating, populated with figures who appear just as lost as the young girl at the heart of them.

As a child, Charles Dodgson would stamp labyrinths into the snow behind his father's rectory, and he included a maze in his homemade magazine, *Mischmasch*, to amuse his three brothers and seven sisters. Unlike most mazes, you start in the centre and try to escape. Adrian Fisher created his own Alice maze in 1991, at Merritown House in Dorset. The centrepiece is the White Rabbit's pocket watch, set permanently to teatime.

At the end of her *Adventures*, Alice wakes up in her older sister's lap. She tells her dream-story and her sister daydreams in turn, imagining Alice as a grown woman.

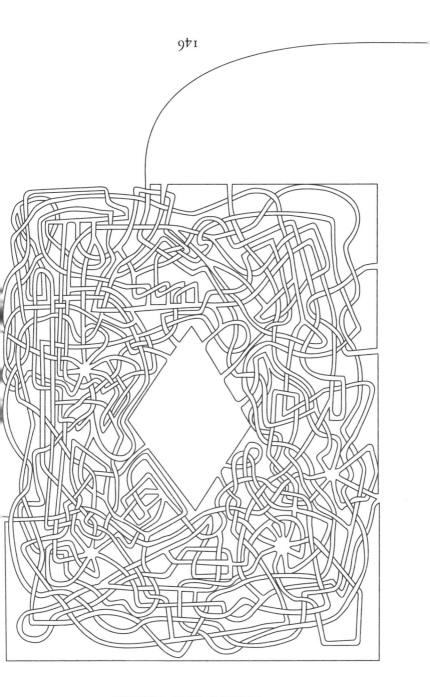

FOLLOW THIS THREAD

The 2006 film *Pan's Labyrinth*, by Guillermo del Toro, draws heavily on *Alice's Adventures in Wonderland*. Its central character is another little girl on the brink of maturity, who retreats into the world of her own imagination in order to make sense of reality.

A fairy, in the shape of an insect, leads Ofelia to an old ruined labyrinth near her stepfather's military headquarters, and her journey into wonderland begins.

'The labyrinth is a very, very powerful sign', explains del Toro. '[. . .] It's about finding, not losing, your way. That was very important for me. It is a place where you do sharp turns and you can have the illusion of being lost, but you are always doing a constant transit to an inevitable centre.'

The opening shot of the film shows Ofelia, lying at the inevitable centre, blood trickling out of her nose. But time is running backwards, and the blood is moving upwards, disappearing, moving from death towards life.

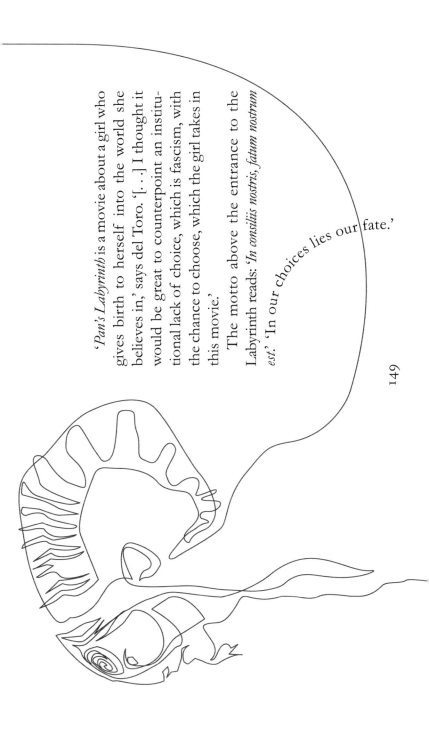

'*Pan's Labyrinth* is a movie about a girl who gives birth to herself into the world she believes in,' says del Toro. '[. . .] I thought it would be great to counterpoint an institutional lack of choice, which is fascism, with the chance to choose, which the girl takes in this movie.'

The motto above the entrance to the Labyrinth reads: '*In consiliis nostris, fatum nostrum est.*' 'In our choices lies our fate.'

Pilgrimage

I give you the end of a golden string,
   Only wind it into a ball,
It will lead you in at Heaven's Gate,
   Built in Jerusalem's wall.

These lines from William Blake's epic prophecy *Jerusalem* recall a popular seventeenth-century copperplate engraving by the Frisian artist Boetius Bolswert. A pilgrim stands at the centre of a maze of raised paths, separated by treacherous crevasses. Elsewhere, lost souls claw the air as they fall into these chasms, but the pilgrim holds a thread that will guide him safely out of the maze. An angel holds the other end, from the top of a heavenly citadel.

St Augustine explained that every Christian is a pilgrim, struggling to find the way to the Lord, in constant danger of stumbling off the righteous path. Francis Quarles, the seventeenth-century English poet, reproduced Bolswert's image in a book of emblems and spelled out its moral:

The World's an intricate Meander,
In which awhile poor Christians wander;
But he who has a heav'nly Ray
To guide him, shall not lose his Way.

'Have you ever heard of the Cretan labyrinth?'

'I have heard something about it,' I replied.

'It was one of the wonders of the world,' he explained, 'a building with so many rooms, compartments and passages that whoever entered it without a guide would wander and grope about without ever finding a way out. But that was a joke compared with the way the labyrinth of this world is arranged, especially in our day.

In *The Labyrinth of the World and Paradise of the Heart*, a seventeenth-century Czech allegory by John Amos Comenius, a pilgrim is lured deeper and deeper into the 'world-city' by two unreliable companions, Ubiquitous, representing human curiosity, and Delusion. The pilgrim is given a pair of spectacles with lenses cut from the glass of presumption and framed with the horn rims of habit, through which he sees the world upside-down. When he finally wrenches them off, he finds himself before a dead-end pit of decay, full of 'worms, frogs, snakes, scorpions, pus and stench'.

Freedom of choice implies the risk of error, and in a world with a strict moral code, that can be a discouraging prospect. Robert Burton laments, in *The Anatomy of Melancholy*, that 'the world itself is a maze, a labyrinth of errors, a desert, a wilderness, a den of thieves, cheaters, etc., full of filthy puddles, horrid rocks, precipitiums, an ocean of adversity, an heavy yoke, wherein infirmities and calamities overtake and follow one another, as the sea-waves'.

Christianity adopted the maze as a symbol of the laborious strictures required by the righteous life, while simultaneously offering a thread to guide believers. 'I am the Way,' Christ told his disciples.

PILGRIMAGE

The most magnificent Christian labyrinth is inside the cathedral of Chartres, which soars above the plain of Beauce in northern France: a Gothic fantasia with a vast rose window, a profusion of flying buttresses and towering, asymmetrical spires. In the thirteenth century, pilgrims from all corners of Europe converged on this cathedral to catch a glimpse of the Sancta Camisa: the tunic worn by the Virgin Mary as she gave birth to Christ, donated to Chartres by Charles the Bald.

On the floor of the nave a 40-foot labyrinth is laid out in blue-black marble.

Anyone entering through the west door becomes entangled in its concentric circles and drawn along its curving, cruciform route to the rosette at the centre. The Christian labyrinth is an evolution of the pattern: it incorporates a cross and increases the number of paths from seven to eleven. Eleven is a sinful number according to Augustine, because it adds to the number of commandments, but falls short of the number of disciples; the labyrinth with eleven paths represents the tangled world of sin.

At the culmination of the Hajj pilgrimage, the faithful make seven turns around the Kaaba.

In the eighteenth century, it was thought that medieval church labyrinths were used to perform symbolic journeys on one's knees, pilgrimages in miniature, substitutes for the arduous journey to Jerusalem. The labyrinth at Reims Cathedral was even known as the Chemin de Jérusalem, the 'Jerusalem Road'.

The Chartres labyrinth recalls the medieval *mappae mundi*, in which Jerusalem was located as the central omphalos or 'navel' of a circular world. The late thirteenth-century *mappa mundi* at Hereford Cathedral even includes a miniature Chartres-type labyrinth on the island of Crete, labelled 'The Labyrinth: that is, the house of Daedalus'.

Church labyrinths also had a ritual signifi-cance. At Easter, a medieval game was played at Auxerre: canons and chaplains joined hands around the perimeter of the labyrinth, while the dean danced a three-step along its path, passing a large leather ball backwards and for-wards to members of the surrounding clergy. Similar Easter celebrations were performed at the cathedrals of Sens and Chartres.

The game's equinoctial timing suggests that the ball represented the sun, its movements relating to the path of the ecliptic and the turn-ing point of the year. It was a celebration of the renewal of spring and, by extension, the resurrection of Christ.

In the Garden of Live Flowers, Alice tries to get to a little hill,
so she takes a path that seems to lead straight there.

'But how curiously it twists! It's more like a corkscrew
than a path! Well, *this* turn goes to the hill, I suppose – no,
it doesn't! This goes straight back to
the house! Well then, I'll try it the
other way.'

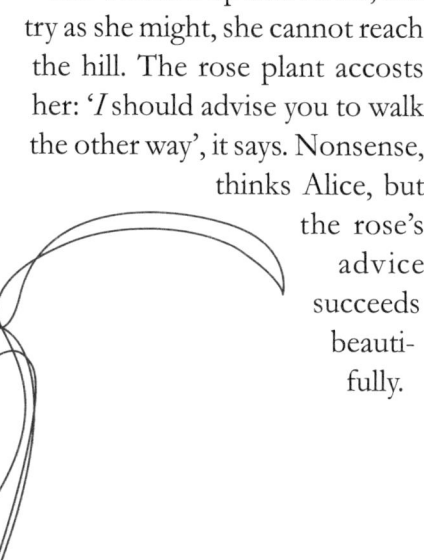

She wanders up and down, but
try as she might, she cannot reach
the hill. The rose plant accosts
her: '*I* should advise you to walk
the other way', it says. Nonsense,
thinks Alice, but
the rose's
advice
succeeds
beauti-
fully.

In
a
maze,
you sometimes need to turn in a counter-intuitive
direction in order to reach the goal. This pendular rhythm
is also present in unicursal labyrinths: Hermann Kern
describes it as 'a chest expanding to inhale'.

'When a person enters a labyrinth, he or she is at first
carried toward the outer edge by a deep breath, so to
speak. After exhaling [. . .] the walker is back near the
middle again. Before inhaling and making a new expansive move, the walker passes near the centre again.'

The movement manifests the *via negativa* of apophatic
theology: progress is possible only through negation.

As St Thomas Aquinas wrote, the most that we can
hope for in our spiritual search for God is 'to know that
we do not know Him'. We arrive at the centre only by
walking the opposite way.

In 1950, Canon Harry Cheales, the rector at Wyck Rissington in Gloucestershire, had a dream in which he was commanded to turn his overgrown garden into a maze.

'It was as though a blank screen appeared before me,' he recalled, 'and a pattern of white light was traced on it like toothpaste from a tube. As soon as it was light, I went outside in my pyjamas and, in fact, I found the traces of a pathway through the thicket exactly as the dream had foretold.'

It took Canon Cheales five years to grow his maze of yew, privet and willow trees. 'Our life is a journey,' he explained. 'The feet and yards of the path through the maze are the months and years of our time. The junctions are the decisions we have to face and the wrong turnings represent the mistakes we make. The centre symbolizes Heaven.'

The maze has since disappeared, but the dream design is recorded in a mosaic on the wall of Wyck Rissington parish church.

The spiritual appeal of labyrinths remains powerful. Canon Lauren Artress, from Grace Church Cathedral in San Francisco, visited Chartres Cathedral in 1991.

She removed the chairs that covered the labyrinth and walked the marble path. These were her first steps on what was to become a personal odyssey to evangelize the meditative and healing power of labyrinths.

'Labyrinths are blueprints for transformation,' she says. 'They release a psychospiritual process of discovery that organically unfolds in our lives.'

On her return home, Artress installed a painted canvas replica of the Chartres labyrinth in the nave of Grace Church Cathedral. On its opening day, people queued for six hours to have the chance of walking it.

Labyrinth walking has now become a regular feature at Grace Church Cathedral. In 1994, the canvas labyrinth was replaced by a tapestry, designed to be walked barefoot. In 2007, a permanent limestone and marble labyrinth was installed.

The Reverend Dr Artress now describes herself as a transpersonal psychotherapist, life coach, spiritual director and Episcopal priest, and she travels the world lecturing on the spiritual benefits of labyrinths.

In 1996, she founded the non-profit organization Veriditas, the World-Wide Labyrinth Project, which aims to 'pepper the planet with labyrinths'. Its database currently lists over 5,200 labyrinths in more than 80 different countries.

On the morning of Good Friday, 6 April 1327, Francesco Petrarch saw a beautiful women in the Church of Saint-Claire in Avignon. He composed a sonnet praising her 'gentle ways' and 'sweet words', which concludes:

> *Mille trecento ventisette, a punto*
> *su l' ora prima, il dí sesto d' aprile,*
> *nel laberinto intrai, né veggio ond' esca.*

> In thirteen twenty-seven, exactly
> at the hour of Prime, on the sixth day of April,
> I entered the labyrinth, and can see no escape.

In this poem, Petrarch brilliantly transmutes the labyrinth metaphor and opens up a whole new world of maze symbolism: he reimagines the pilgrim's path as the course of romantic love.

'Labyrinths of Love' became immensely popular in Europe between the mid-sixteenth and mid-seventeenth centuries. They could represent either the happy outcome of a circuitous courtship, or the reverse: the inescapability of an unwanted entanglement.

In an eighteenth-century engraving by Hieronymus Sperling, a naked cherub rushes eagerly into a maze of love, but in the central panel he is blindfolded and lost, and when he eventually tries to disentangle himself on the right, he is held back by swathes of brambles.

After an anxious day and night's sailing, Theseus and Ariadne, and the crew of Athenians, beach their ship on the island of Dia, known today as Naxos.

Exhausted, they spill on to the beach, digging their fingers into the hot, white sand, lying back and looking up to the sky and sending thanks to blazing Apollo. Theseus crouches in the surf, letting the clear wavelets run in and out of his open hand, acknowledging Poseidon likewise.

They spend the day resting, regaining their strength and scouting for food. One of the Athenians catches a young pig in the woods, and in the evening they light a fire on the beach and cook the meat.

After eating, the Athenians sleep where they have been sitting. As the flames die and the embers start to glow, Theseus and Ariadne steal away from the fire. They find a clearing out of sight of the beach. There are shadowy structures nearby in the darkness, but their eyes and hands are for each other only. They whisper vows in each other's ears as they come together with all the pent-up relief of their escape from Crete and the Labyrinth.

.

When Ariadne wakes, she is alone. The sun is newly up. She looks around sleepily. She is lying at the edge of a small temple sanctuary. She feels the rumpled ground where Theseus lay beside her. She sits up a little. The sanctuary bears the emblems of the god Dionysus. She looks at the glancing light slanting between the columns. She becomes aware of sounds in the distance, shouts and splashes.

She is standing and running towards the beach. She clears the trees and sees the ship in the water, the last of the Athenians jumping aboard. They are leaving without her. The wind ruffles and bellies the sails as she runs down the sand. She splashes into the shallows but the boat is gathering speed and she can't wade fast enough to catch it.

Theseus stands in the stern. Ariadne stops, with all the dignity of a priestess of Crete, and they hold each other's eyes. She continues to stand in the surf, long after the ship has disappeared beyond the horizon.

The morning sun shines on the shifting ebbs, flows, channels and currents, some running back to Knossos, others leading her lover away from her.

The air feels cold.

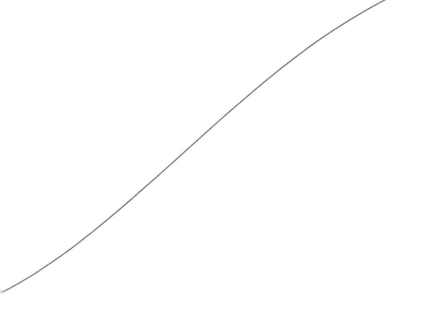

No one knows why Theseus abandoned Ariadne.

Some say it was a freak of the weather: that Ariadne was put ashore first and the wind forced the ship back to sea. Others say that Theseus's love had alighted elsewhere, that Phaedra, Ariadne's prettier younger sister, was his mistress before they even arrived at Naxos.

Another story tells how the god Dionysus appeared to Theseus while he slept beside Ariadne. Dionysus, the horned god of wine and religious ecstasy, the god worshipped in frenzy, stood before him in a dream. He was angry that his sanctuary had been defiled, and in recompense he demanded Ariadne for himself.

Whatever the case, when Ariadne found herself alone on the shore, she cried aloud for vengeance, remembering everything she had done for love of Theseus: how she had deceived her father, abetted her brother's murder, abandoned her motherland. All this to be deserted now.

As she sat on the sand, Dionysus approached from the woods, with his train of maenads and satyrs, and the god took her to be his bride. He gave her a diadem, crafted out of blue gold and jewels from India, and carried her up to the heavens.

Ariadne's crown is still visible, shining in the night sky as the constellation Corona Borealis, the Crown of the North Wind.

In Mary Renault's rendering of the myth, Naxos is the site of a Dionysian cult. Theseus and Ariadne attend a Bacchic ritual, and watch maenads, dressed in animal masks, carry the young Naxian king up the sacred mountain. Ariadne is infected by the fervour of the crowd and swept along until Theseus loses her in the frenzy. He follows, enjoying the revels himself, becoming increasingly inebriated.

The whole drunken crowd is possessed by the spirit of the god, and Theseus finds himself making love to two Naxian girls in a clearing below the snow line, dimly aware of distant, escalating shrieks.

He doesn't find Ariadne again until the evening.

'Her eyelids lay smooth and full and glossy over her eyes, and against the dark lashes her cheek bloomed softly. By those I knew her, and by the tender breast cradled upon her arm. I could not see her mouth, for the blood all over it. It was open, for she was breathing heavily; I saw her teeth, even, crusted with dried blood. As I bent over her, its stale reek met me mixed with the smell of wine.'

Still sleeping, Ariadne opens her sticky palm and reveals something too gory to name, some horrifying body part of the king who died in the mountains, ripped to pieces in the frenzied orgy.

Theseus, lost in horror, cannot recover his love for Ariadne, and he abandons her to be a priestess to Dionysus.

Michel Foucault called mazes 'theatres of Dionysian castration'.

One of Shakespeare's two plays about Theseus opens a few days before his marriage to Hippolyta, the Amazon queen.

'I woo'd thee with my sword, / And won thy love, doing thee injuries,' he says to her; 'But I will wed thee in another key, / With pomp, with triumph and with revelling,'

Meanwhile, in the twilit woods outside Athens, Oberon accuses Titania of having made Theseus 'break his faith' with Ariadne.

A Midsummer Night's Dream is a maze-like play. Bottom the weaver is a comical Minotaur. Around him, four Athenian lovers are led 'up and down, up and down', until they are 'amazedly' lost in the woods, their affections switching radically from one to another while they sleep.

As Lysander says, 'The course of true love never did run smooth.'

Nothing is what it seems, and the accustomed order is repeatedly overturned. Even 'the quaint mazes in the wanton green,' exclaims Titania, 'For lack of tread are undistinguishable'.

Titania's 'quaint mazes' are the turf mazes that were once familiar features of village greens in England. They are labyrinths cut into the soil, leaving either a raised grassy pathway or a sunken earthy path between turf walls.

Eight ancient turf mazes have survived in England, and a handful of others in Germany and Scandinavia. The largest English turf maze is on the town common in Saffron Walden. Its design incorporates protrusions or 'bastions' at its four corners. The central mound once sported an ash tree, but it burned down on Bonfire Night, 1823.

Traditionally, turf mazes have been the rendezvous for amorous activities. An eighteenth-century account describes how the Saffron Walden maze was 'used by the beaux and belles of the town, a young

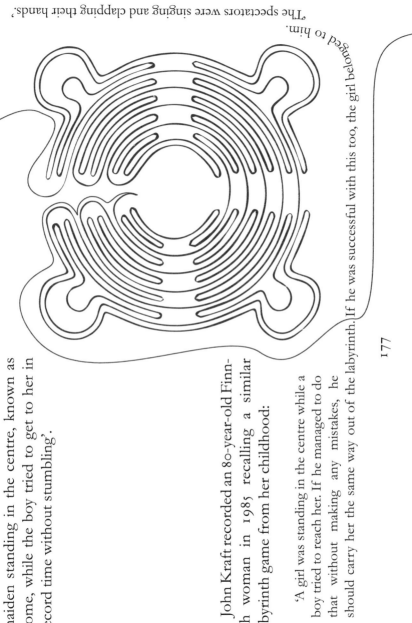

maiden standing in the centre, known as home, while the boy tried to get to her in record time without stumbling'.

John Kraft recorded an 80-year-old Finnish woman in 1985 recalling a similar labyrinth game from her childhood:

'A girl was standing in the centre while a boy tried to reach her. If he managed to do that without making any mistakes, he should carry her the same way out of the labyrinth. If he was successful with this too, the girl belonged to him.

Mazes have also been the setting for more debauched activities.

The original maze at Schloß Schönbrunn in Vienna, for instance, was destroyed, according to Giovanni Mariotti, because it had become the habitual rendezvous for 'soldiers and maids, officers and gentlewomen, prostitutes and gentlemen'. Similarly, during orgiastic eighteenth-century parties at Villa Pisani near Stra, a blindfolded woman would stand at the top of a central tower and give herself to the first man to reach her.

'So, Cynthia, have you seen the hedge maze?'

'Well, I came through it.'

'Yes, but there's an intriguing little bower in the corner. Had you seen that before?'

'No.'

'Would you let me show you? It's so amusing.'

As Adrian Fisher showed me around his maze, he began

to perform a dramatic sketch, taking both roles himself. He had already told me his maze was a 'party machine' and now he was imagining the soirée in full swing.

'You go there, you see, and you sit on the little bench, you and Cynthia, and your hand sort of – strokes her knee,' he explained.

'And it's terribly exciting and terribly tame and terribly safe, because any moment your chums could come round the corner:

'"Oh, Pongo! That's where you are! Oh yes, I thought you'd find Cynthia. Ooh – you want to watch out for his fondering fingers. What fun! Has he stolen a kiss yet? Who cares?"

'The point is,' Adrian laughed, 'nothing dreadful's going to happen, because you could be discovered at any time – but equally, you might not.

'It's terribly romantic.'

I found Greg.

I was put in touch with a professor at York St John University, by an art gallery in the city that had exhibited paintings by a Greg Bright.

'When I visited Greg recently to pick-up the artworks,' the professor told me, '[. . .] I was the first person to cross his threshold in the seventeen years since I moved him into his house.'

The professor had once been the guitarist in Greg's experimental rock band, Silent Sister, and they had stayed in touch. I asked if he thought Greg would meet us. 'I think you stand little chance. Greg is firstly extremely reclusive and secondly despises mazes.'

'I've just had a long telephone conversation with Greg,' he wrote later that day, 'and, as I feared, he politely declined your offer. He wanted me to clarify that he does not despise mazes but just the attention they arouse and the subsequent attention on him. As it stands, I don't think there is any possibility of meeting with Greg at the moment.'

I caught a train to the sea, and then a branch line, and finally walked up a steep hill to a circle of residential houses. Some were positioned below the level of the road, almost out of sight behind skips of scrap metal and gutted car chassis. The house was obscured by a wild front garden with unkempt bushes, sycamore trees and mounds of ivy spilling over the low brick wall on to the pavement.

I stepped down the narrow jungly path and rang the bell.

And the Maze King opened the door.

He was tall, 60, with a long face and a commanding nose. He had thin hair, past his shoulders, and wore a torn black leather jacket over a white-collared shirt.

I had persuaded the professor to vet me at a wharf-side café in Bristol, and Greg had finally agreed to meet.

I spent an afternoon with him and he described his new method of painting and showed me sections of a vast fragmentary novel-in-progress about a semi-autobiographical character named Llabrys: 'Concomitant with the fragmentary nature, which seems as much endemic as

contingent,' he explained, 'the chapters are highly autonomous and heterogeneous, not to mention heteroclitic.'

In all his work, Greg imposes constraints on himself.

'If there's no law, there's no tension with the law,' he said, 'so one thing is as good as another, there's no hierarchy any more. Whereas if you negotiate these difficult constraints, then something is accomplished by that negotiation.

'It's like with Bach,' he continued, recalling the sound of the music with his hands: 'what, for me, Bach does, is make the law sound like freedom.'

Freedom

On the voyage from Naxos, on the way home to Athens, Theseus and his companions put in at the holy island of Delos, the birthplace of Apollo.

They sacrifice to the god and begin to dance. They dance out of reverence, they dance out of gratitude, they dance for joy and for sorrow, they dance for forgiveness, they dance for dancing's sake and they dance for freedom. Their dance is ecstatic, freeing themselves from their selves, expressing their common bond.

'The essence of the labyrinth is not its outward form, its delineating stones and hedges,' writes Jill Purce in *The Mystic Spiral*, 'but the movement it engenders. The spiral, mandalic movements of the dance predate even the labyrinth itself.'

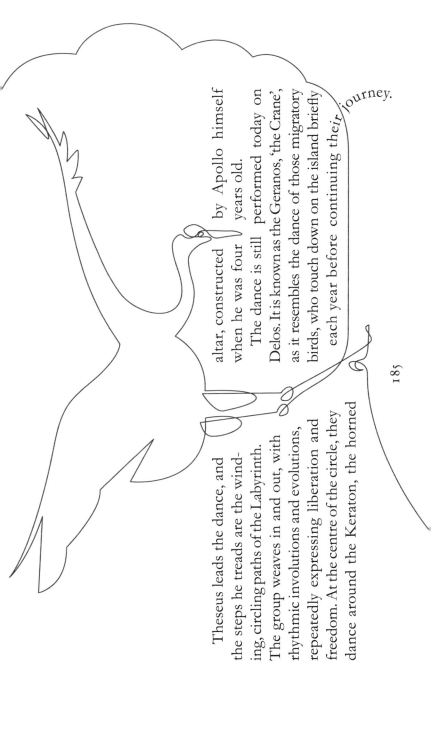

Theseus leads the dance, and the steps he treads are the winding, circling paths of the Labyrinth. The group weaves in and out, with rhythmic involutions and evolutions, repeatedly expressing liberation and freedom. At the centre of the circle, they dance around the Keraton, the horned altar, constructed by Apollo himself when he was four years old.

The dance is still performed today on Delos. It is known as the Geranos, 'the Crane', as it resembles the dance of those migratory birds, who touch down on the island briefly each year before continuing their journey.

'Unless you err,' says the devil Mephistopheles in Goethe's *Faust*, 'naught can be truly known.'

The pleasure of mazes, or *irrgärten* as they are called in German, is not in being lost but in what is found through being lost. If you surrender yourself to the maze, you stop worrying about finding the correct way and there is a liberating, euphoric sense of freedom.

'Not till we are lost, in other words not till we have lost the world,' wrote Henry David Thoreau in *Walden*, 'do we begin to find ourselves, and realize where we are and the infinite extent of our relations.'

Through being lost we become better aware of ourselves. The process is not straightforward: letting go entails a physical and mental journey, through error, fear and self-acknowledgement. 'The right way to wholeness is made up, unfortunately, of fateful detours and wrong turnings,' wrote Carl Jung. 'It is a *longissima via*, not straight but snakelike [. . .] whose labyrinthine twists and turns are not lacking in terrors.'

They are approaching Athens. Theseus stands at the prow of the Cretan ship as the city appears on the horizon. He is the returning hero. He has broken the Labyrinth, killed the Minotaur, released his people from their deadly tribute. His head is giddy with homecoming.

Above the city he sees the acropolis and the royal palace. He is full of exultation, urging the ship to speed through the water, willing the space between himself and the shore to shrink to nothing.

It seems an age since he left. It cannot be more than six months, but he has grown, changed from a boy into a man, a worthy heir to his father.

Finally, they reach the harbour walls at Phalerum, expecting joyous, welcoming crowds, but instead they meet a people in mourning, wailing and crying, beating their breasts.

The king is dead.

Only then does Theseus remember his promise to Aegeus. He looks up at the black canvas sails fluttering above him and in his mind's eye he sees his father, straining from the acropolis for a sign of his son. Today his wait came to an end.

Aegeus saw the sails and cast himself down from the high rock. He fell like a stone, dashed into the foaming waves, and to this day the Aegean Sea bears his name.

Theseus steps off the ship, his mouth dry. He is the new king of Athens, but he can think only of his own forgetfulness and the swift vengeance of a slighted priestess, standing in the shallows of Naxos.

On Crete, Minos knows who is responsible for the disappearance of his daughter. Only one man knows the secrets of the Labyrinth: the same man who built it, the same man who enabled his wife's bestial act, the same man who created the Minotaur in the first place.

Minos throws Daedalus into his own Labyrinth, with his son, Icarus. The master craftsman finds himself trapped in the maze of his own making, no longer the outsider, the observer, the artist.

His mind is already working. He knows there are sections of the Labyrinth that are open to the sky. Taking the young Icarus by the hand, he leads him to a place where they can see the heavens and breathe fresh air.

He has been making a study of birds in flight, how they use the wind, how they angle their bodies and shape their wings. While Icarus sits cross-legged, looking up to Apollo, Daedalus starts work. During the daytime he traps birds with a leather thong. He breaks their necks and spends the evenings plucking. He fetches materials: reeds, pliable wood, twine and balls of wax. The hidden stores have lain untouched since the days of the Labyrinth's construction.

As he works, Icarus plays around him, throwing feathers into the air and laughing as they flutter down, stealing globs of wax and moulding them warm with his fingers.

When Daedalus is finished, the feathers are lined in supple curves, each fixed in two places with twine and wax.

He fits his own wings first, and then helps Icarus with his.

He places his hands on his son's shoulders. 'Fly the middle course, my son. Do not soar too high, or the fire will burn your wings; do not swoop too low, or the feathers will be wetted in the sea.' His eyes glisten as he looks into Icarus's eager face, searching to see if his words have landed safely.

Father and son stand apart, and with a mighty effort, with excitement and trepidation, they crouch and launch together into the air, the first mortals ever to escape the earth.

With birds' eyes they see the Labyrinth from above, the privileged view of the gods.

194

At first they are clumsy and faltering, learning gradually how to adjust their wings, understanding how to read the currents and thermals of the air, but increasingly they grow confident, striking out across the sea, laughing at their newfound freedom, swooping and loop-the-looping and calling to each other.

FREEDOM

For the first time they see whole islands surrounded by water, they spot people in miniature and ships and towns. Below the water's surface they see dark shoals of fish, and in the distance the smoke trails of temple fires. They pass Paros and Delos on their left, then Lebinthus, and Calymne, the honey isle. They pass Samos on their right and Icarus laughs as he climbs higher.

Fishermen, ploughmen and shepherds look up and shade their eyes, witnessing gods.

195

The gods of the Nazca people in Peru have a particularly spectacular view. The Nazca Lines cover 170 square miles of a windless plateau below the Andes. They are shallow lines, formed by clearing the brown, oxidized stones away from the desiccated pampas, revealing the pale clay underneath.

The Nazca people created these lines between 500 BCE and 500 CE. They managed to clear perfectly straight lines stretching up to nine miles across the plain, as well as vast, intricate zoomorphic figures. Most of the designs consist of a single line that curls into spirals and angular, figurative forms, without ever crossing itself or making a dead end.

One of the designs is a three-path labyrinth; or rather, the route through a three-path labyrinth. How the labyrinth symbol reached such a remote part of South America is unknown.

The Nazca Lines are too big to see properly from the ground. Juddering seven-seater aeroplanes drag tourists up into the air for the gods'-eye view.

Like the Nazca Lines, the most prolific maze-form in the world today is best appreciated from above.

Maize mazes are formed by creating paths through cornfields. The advantage of maize is that it grows quickly, unlike yew. The mazes only last for one summer, but they can be extremely lucrative in that time, and at the end of the season the crop is harvested as usual.

Adrian Fisher designed the first maize maze in 1993, at Annville, Pennsylvania: it was a stegosaurus, inspired by *Jurassic Park*, which was released the same year.

Maize mazes often have elaborate figurative designs, which make excellent aerial photographs and provide opportunities for coordinated merchandise. Fisher calls them 'marketing machines'.

Six times Fisher has broken the Guinness World Record for the largest maize maze in the world, 'the horticultural equivalent of the America's Cup'.

Recently, the Italian publisher Franco Maria Ricci completed the world's largest bamboo maze outside Parma: Il Labirinto della Masone. At the centre is a museum for his art collection and a library of rare books. Many years ago, when he was first contemplating the project, he walked around the site with his friend Jorge Luis Borges, explaining how large it would be, but the writer was unimpressed.

'Borges objected,' recalls Ricci, '[. . .] saying that the largest labyrinth in the world already existed. It was the desert.'

In 'The Two Kings and the Two Labyrinths', Borges imagines a maze maker, abandoned three days' ride into a desert, where there are 'no stairways to climb, nor doors to force, nor wearying galleries to wander through, nor walls'.

The constraints of a maze provide something tangible against which to pit your wits; a labyrinth with no walls has too much freedom; it would drive you mad. It recalls Captain Ahab, poring over charts of the four oceans, 'threading a maze of currents and eddies'.

'There's no need to build a labyrinth,' Borges writes, 'when the entire universe is one.'

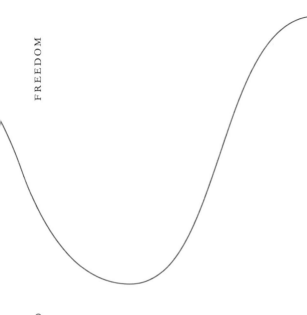

'I met him a couple of times,' said Adrian Fisher, when I asked him about Greg Bright. 'He only built a couple of mazes ever. But he did do the one at Longleat, and it is quite ingenious.'

Fisher thinks Greg's maze is an inadequate visitor experience. 'Longleat needs more space. It needs wider paths. It needs special spaces where you can experience different things.'

'It goes on for an hour and a half, and that's not funny' Fisher told Julian Barnes in 1991. 'It doesn't vary its pace . . . there's an utter contempt for the market.'

Adrian has, in fact, been brought in to 'improve' Greg Bright's maze at Longleat: he has installed 'Lift if Lost' panels with helpful arrows and he has created a quick exit route from the central tower, across a newly installed bridge.

Tim Bentley, the Estates Manager at Longleat, had originally suggested these alterations to Greg, but he wasn't keen. 'He thought going through a maze should be, and would most likely be, a fairly painful experience,' Bentley recalled.

'Frivolity is a major gangrene of the psyche,' says Greg. '[. . .] I have never been complicit with the "fun and games" angle.'

William Blake called the human mind 'the infinite labyrinth.'

The unnamed narrator of W. G. Sebald's *Rings of Saturn* visits the Somerleyton Hall maze. This nineteenth-century yew maze, which is still open to the public, has generous gravel paths, elegantly curved hedges and a central knoll topped with a small pagoda. The maze's proportions are gracious and welcoming, but the narrator gets utterly lost. In the end, he resorts to scoring lines in the sand with the heel of his boot at the entrance to each dead-end passage before he can finally escape.

The tone of Sebald's fictionalized pilgrimage is gloomily saturnine. The narrator drifts through Suffolk, connecting remnants of deliquescent worlds: the pier at Lowestoft, the Sailors' Reading Room at Southwold, the vanishing village of Dunwich. His mind wanders too, from one subject to another, orbiting, like the fragments of a shattered moon, his own mortality. The skull-shaped maze at Somerleyton Hall comes to represent his pilgrimage in microcosm: his mind adrift, trapped within his own pate, anticipating dead ends.

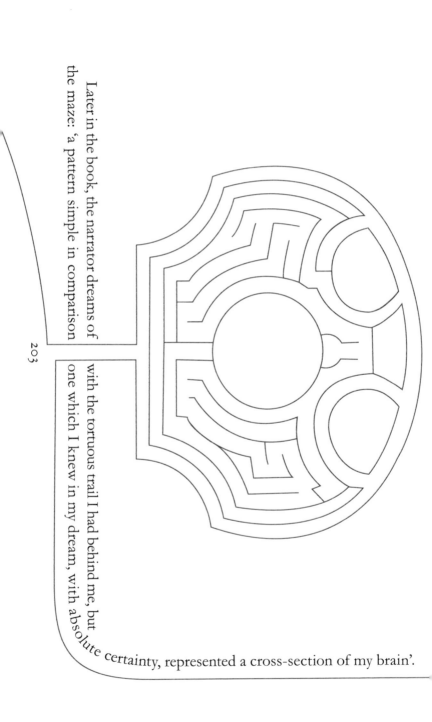

Later in the book, the narrator dreams of the maze: 'a pattern simple in comparison with the tortuous trail I had behind me, but one which I knew in my dream, with absolute certainty, represented a cross-section of my brain'.

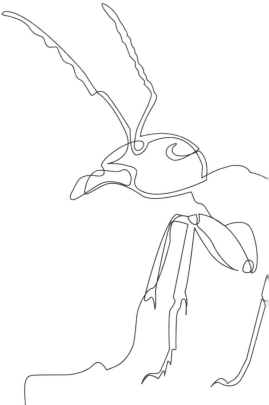

Michael Ayrton imagined that when Daedalus landed at Cumae and collapsed, he fell on to an anthill.

'An ant [. . .] entered my head through a nostril and, undislodged by sneezing, went in panic deep into my brain. Painless to me, once past my itching mucous-membrane, he passed into my mind.'

Our brains contain up to 100 billion neurons, with rhizomic synapse connections that are continually forming and dissolving. Electrical impulses run around this vast network like ants.

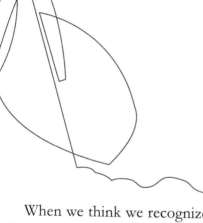

When we think we recognize a stranger in the street, for example, our mind has quite literally lost its way. Researchers at John Hopkins University have shown that the hippocampus is responsible for cross-checking the faces we pass. It triggers a series of 'checks' or decision junctions: the brain asks, are you sure? Are you sure you're sure? And if the electrical signals take the wrong turning too many times, we smile and wave, until the stranger's puzzled face overrides the system and we flood with embarrassment.

The interior of Greg's house was ascetic. He led me through to the back room.

'This represents, really, the acme of my maze drawings,' he said, introducing an enormous piece of paper that filled an entire wall. It showed a vast circle of tangled, overlapping paths, ending in hundreds of circular nodes. It was recognizable as a maze, but only just: it was a wild design, crammed with exuberant strokes that went nowhere, painstaking diversions around invisible shapes, partial-valve spirals with paths that either spun out of control or stopped dead. It was the third iteration of what Greg called his 'Ghost Telepoint Mazes'.

He explained how the design was constructed following a set of rules, involving four weights of path, hypothetical 'triskeles' or triple spirals, and 'telepoints', nodes between which the visible path 'teleports'. 'There's no way of recovering the underlying network of this,' said Greg, scanning the surface of the paper. 'It remains ultimately cryptic from that point of view.'

When paths met the edges of the circle, they reappeared on the opposite side.

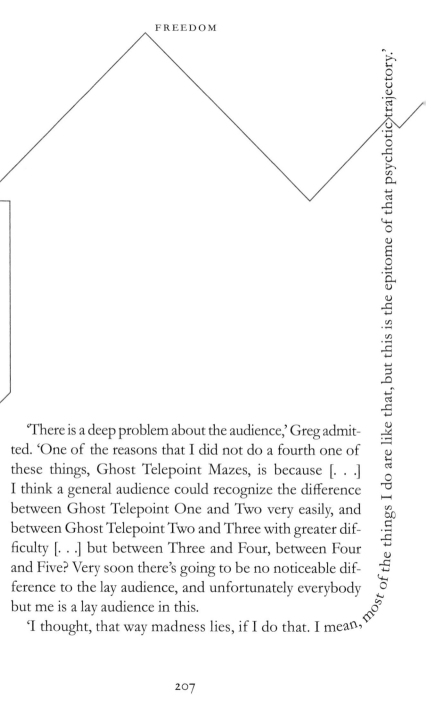

'...but this is the epitome of that psychotic trajectory.'

'...most of the things I do are like that,

'There is a deep problem about the audience,' Greg admitted. 'One of the reasons that I did not do a fourth one of these things, Ghost Telepoint Mazes, is because [. . .] I think a general audience could recognize the difference between Ghost Telepoint One and Two very easily, and between Ghost Telepoint Two and Three with greater difficulty [. . .] but between Three and Four, between Four and Five? Very soon there's going to be no noticeable difference to the lay audience, and unfortunately everybody but me is a lay audience in this.

'I thought, that way madness lies, if I do that. I mean,

In Kafka's story 'The Burrow', an unidentified mustelid constructs an intricate underground sett for itself, with labyrinthine defences and elaborate decoy entrances.

The creature becomes increasingly paranoid. He is convinced a predator might stumble across his disguised entrance, or that a malicious enemy is burrowing through the bowels of the earth towards the innermost chamber where he lives.

He has constructed the outer windings of his burrow to form 'a whole little maze of passages' to trap intruders. The design of this outer labyrinth is 'theoretically brilliant', he allows, but he now sees it only as a 'flimsy piece of jugglery', the mere thought of which agonizes him.

'I must thread the tormenting complica-
tions of this labyrinth physically as well as
mentally whenever I go out, and I am both
exasperated and touched when, as sometimes happens, I lose myself for a moment
in my own maze.'

William Kurelek was a Canadian artist who struggled with mental illness throughout his life. While being treated in the Maudsley Hospital in London in 1953, he painted *The Maze*, which is now on display at the Bethlem Museum of the Mind in Beckenham.

It shows a man's skull, split open and hinged forwards to reveal a network of interconnected rooms. In the central chamber lies a rat.

'The white rat curled up in the central cavity represents my spirit (I suppose),' Kurelek explained. 'He is curled up with frustration from having run the passages so long without hope of escaping out of this maze of unhappy thoughts.'

'He just looked so completely lost,' says one of Kurelek's doctors in a clip of documentary footage. 'I've never seen anyone quite so lost as he was.'

In 1971, after his condition improved and he was out of hospital, Kurelek painted *Out of the Maze*, a companion piece that is also on display in Beckenham. The claustrophobia of *The Maze* is replaced by an open and expansive scene of a family picnic in a field near an unruffled pond, with a few docile cows and a single red car passing by.

Looking closer, however, we see that the maze-skull is still cracked open and lying amongst the grass in the bottom left corner, and on the horizon a dark storm is gathering.

One of the most iconic representations of madness on screen is presented in Stanley Kubrick's film adaptation of *The Shining*.

Wendy and Danny explore the Overlook Maze: they wander around corners, in and out of dead ends and past long-perspective passages. The picture fades to Jack slouching through the Overlook Hotel, towards an architectural model of the maze.

He looks over it, and we cut to a bird's-eye view of a different, vastly complicated maze, bigger than the edges of the screen, as ominous music plays and we see the small figures of Danny and Wendy arriving at the centre.

'I didn't think it was going to be this big, did you?' asks Wendy.

The Overlook Hotel, and its labyrinthine, intricately carpeted corridors, externalize Jack's broiling mind. 'This whole place is such an enormous maze,' says Wendy when she is being shown around.

The hotel traps and possesses spirits within its walls, from its foundations on a Native American burial ground, to the ghosts of the Grady twins, slaughtered by their father.

As Jack loses himself inside the Overlook, he ends up bellowing through the literal hedge maze, hell-bent on murdering his own son.

FREEDOM

As king of Athens, Theseus united the Attic city-states.

The ecstatic dance on Delos had shown him the power of the *demos*, of a common cause, and he set about creating the world's first democracy.

He went from town to town, persuading every chief to join him, promising to be king in time of war only, and otherwise a guardian of common law at a central council chamber. He instituted a Panathenaic Games, to be held every four years, and he established the Festival of the Grape Boughs, in honour of Dionysus and Ariadne. He married Phaedra, Ariadne's sister, to ensure peace with Crete, but his true affections were devoted to the memory of Hippolyta, his Amazonian queen. He named their son Hippolytus, after his mother.

Theseus must have felt that his life's work was all but done. But the wheel had not quite turned.

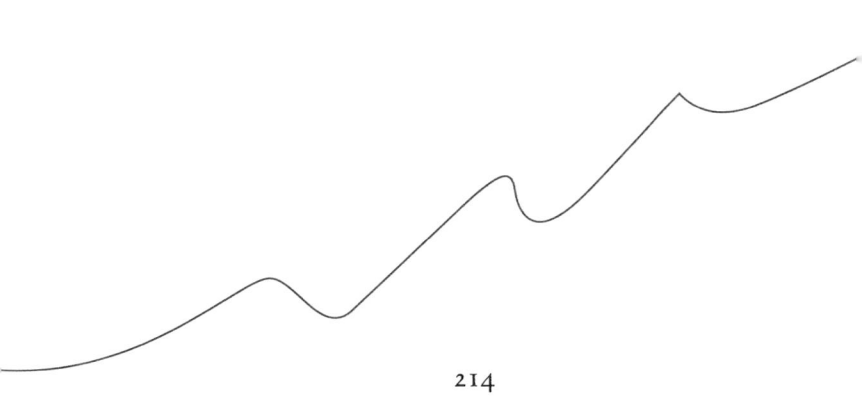

Phaedra developed an interest in her stepson, Hippolytus, which grew into a passion. Like her mother before her, she was gripped by an unnatural lust. One night, Phaedra feigned sickness and called the handsome Hippolytus to attend her bedside. When he came, she implored him to lie with her.

Shocked, Hippolytus fled, and Phaedra, afraid of Theseus's wrath, acted quickly. She tore her own clothes and threw open the doors to her rooms, accusing Hippolytus of attempted incest and rape. Theseus believed her and prayed to Poseidon to punish his son.

Hippolytus was riding the sea road in his chariot. A gleaming white bull came trotting out of the waves in front of his horses, which shied and overturned his chariot. Unable to free himself from the reins, Hippolytus was pulled along by the snarling horses and dragged to his death on the bumpy road.

Our perception of reality is based on shadows, thrown on to the wall in front of us. It is the role of the philosopher to break free, says Plato, and struggle out of the cave, 'up a steep and rugged ascent' into the sunshine. There, once the philosopher's eyes have grown accustomed to the light, he will perceive truth and the nature of reality.

Knowledge alone will not be enough, however: the philosopher will wish to return and emancipate his fellows. But when he returns to the cave, he will not be able to see so well in the darkness.

'There will be many jokes about the man who went on a visit to the sun and lost his eyes,' writes Plato, and if the philosopher is subsequently discovered trying to enlighten anyone, the intolerant cave dwellers will execute him.

Leaving a labyrinth is dangerous. Perhaps it would be safer to stay inside, to turn back into the comforting corridors, not to risk stepping outside the walls.

I said goodbye and Greg closed the stippled-glass door. His blurry figure receded down the hall, and I made my way back up the overgrown garden.

In André Gide's novella *Thésée*, Daedalus reveals his ultimate secret:

'To keep anyone in the labyrinth, the best thing was to ensure, not so much that he would not be able to leave [...] but that he would not wish to leave.'

Mouth

Theseus's ship, with its black sails, remained in the harbour at Phalerum long after his death. Every time one of the old planks decayed, it was replaced; when the sails developed mildew, new sails were fitted; when the ropes gave out, modern sheets were added. Gradually the entire ship was replaced piece for piece, until nothing of the original remained, and now the vessel presents a paradox: is it the same ship on which Theseus returned from Crete, or a different one?

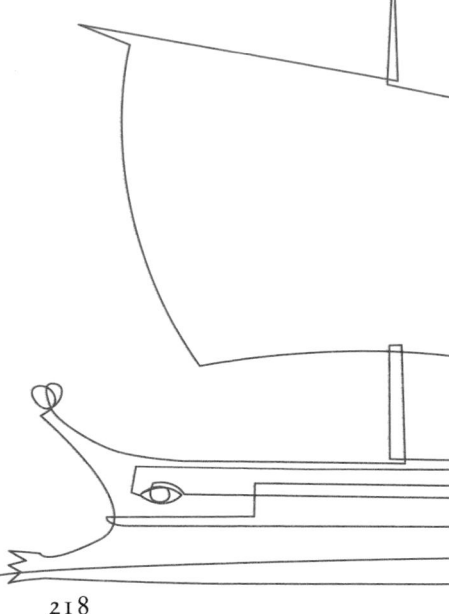

The same question might be asked of mazes: to what extent do meanings persist through the changing forms of labyrinths and mazes, and the myriad stories we tell about them?

Like all works of art, a maze is a conversation: an exposition by the maker and a response from the walker. Each encounter with a maze is different, but the meeting always acts as a mirror: you emerge with a better knowledge of yourself.

Virgil tells us that Daedalus was unable to craft the last panel of the Cumaean Gates: twice he lifted his tools to depict the fall of Icarus; twice his hands fell to his sides. No doubt the memory of his son's death was painful, but he might also have been tasting the bitterness of irony.

In his youth, in Athens, Daedalus had taken his nephew, Talos, as his apprentice. Talos lacked Daedalus's technical skill, but his young mind thrilled with inspiration, and each spark of the apprentice's creativity dripped jealousy into Daedalus's stomach.

When Talos, fiddling with a fish's jawbone, discovered its application as a pair of compasses, inventing the first device for tracing a perfect circle, the storm of Daedalus's envy broke. He pushed Talos off the Athenian acropolis and the boy dropped like a stone, through fathoms of air, disappearing into a sea of jagged rocks.

Though some say the gods took pity on Talos, just before impact, and turned him into a partridge.

Daedalus fled the murder, and wandered foreign shores, claiming Talos's inventions as his own.

Thinking himself safely lost, he found himself under the royal patronage of the House of Minos, and made his home there, until the double spiral of his fate began to coil back on itself.

On Michael Ayrton's gravestone in Hadstock church-yard in Essex, his epitaph is a three-dimensional replica of his maze at Arkville.

'Within the great maze of a man's life are many smaller ones, each seemingly complete in itself,' he wrote in *The Maze Maker*, 'and in passing through each one he dies in part, for in each he leaves behind him a part of his life and it lies dead behind him. It is a paradox of the labyrinth that its centre appears to be the way to freedom.'

Till I beheld through a round aperture
Some of the beauteous things that Heaven doth bear;
Thence we came forth to rebehold the stars.

—Dante

Acknowledgements

Many people have generously helped to guide this book's convolutions. First and foremost is Tom Kingsley, with whom I spent three weeks driving from maze to maze and meeting maze makers. As always, Tom has been a fount of ideas and encouragement throughout. One day we plan to – we will – make our own maze. Many thanks also to Patrick Kingsley and Matt Lloyd-Rose, who joined that trip, and to all the people who spoke to us: Lord Bath of Longleat; Stan Beckensell; Tim Bentley; Greg Bright; Gill Brown; Clarissa Cochran; Michael Eavis; Adrian Fisher, Adrian Fisher Ltd; Lindsey Heyes, Symonds Yat; Justine Hopkins; Graham King, Museum of Witchcraft; Prudence Jones; Gary Peters; Jeff Saward, Labyrinthos; Jan Sellers; Pat Welch; Barbara Wilcox and the Saffron Walden Maze Festival team.

More recently, it has been a delight to collaborate with the single-line genius Quibe, Christophe Louis, who manages to capture the essence of an image with minimum ink, and the legendary designer Jim Stoddart, who sculpted this extraordinary-looking book, recreating the twists and turns of the classical labyrinth (see page 11) with the shifting page orientations. I am hugely grateful to Cecilia Stein and Helen Conford at Particular Books, consummate and patient editors, the sharp eyes of Rebecca Lee, Emma Horton and Kit Shepherd, and the publicity and marketing nous of Etty Eastwood and Julie Woon. As ever, my brilliant agent Patrick Walsh has offered advice and enthusiasm from the start, ably assisted by John Ash.

I owe a huge debt of gratitude to three friends in particular, who provide constant support: Matt Lloyd-Rose, Ed Posnett and Andy Wimbush. Thank you for the long discussions on Jura and for all the encouragement since. Special thanks also to Ben Taylor, for the winter's walk when we discussed rats. Thank you to my parents and sister Georgina, who have put up with mazes for a while now; I trace my fixation to the turf mizmaze on St Catherine's Hill near Winchester, which we used to visit most Sundays. And finally, thank you to Georgie, with whom I am so glad to be lost in this most enjoyable, exciting and surprising of mazes.

And one last one: thanks to Jorge Luis Borges, the blind Argentine librarian, who did most of the best thinking about mazes and labyrinths, who saw the entire world as a labyrinth, a vast labyrinth of labyrinths, 'one sinuous spreading labyrinth that would encompass the past and the future and in some way involve the stars'.

A List of Mazes

Page numbers in bold refer to illustrations.

Upright Mazes

Alice in Wonderland Maze, The Merritown House, Dorset	Adrian Fisher	147
Alice's Curious Labyrinth Disneyland Paris, France	Walt Disney Imagineering	147
Annville maize maze [lost] Annville, Pennsylvania	Adrian Fisher	198
Arkville Maze Arkville, New York State	Michael Ayrton	136, **137**, 222
Château de Baugé [lost] Baugé-en-Anjou, France	unknown	14
Chevening House Chevening, Kent	Philip Henry Stanhope	20, **21**
Crocodilopolis mausoleum [lost] Faiyum, Egypt	Amenemhat III	88, **89**
Edinburgh Zoo (The Darwin Maze) Edinburgh, Scotland	Adrian Fisher	145
Forbidden Corner, The Tupgill Park, North Yorkshire	Colin Armstrong	5
Glacier Garden mirror maze (the Alhambra) Lucerne, Switzerland	Gustav Castan	120
Hampton Court Maze Hampton Court Palace, Surrey	George London and Henry Wise	16, **17**, 18–19, 60
Hôtel des Tournelles [lost] Paris, France	unknown	14
Imprint of Man Lechlade Mill, Gloucestershire	Randoll Coate	**68**
Japanese panel mazes Japan	Stuart Landsborough	69
Laberinto de Borges, El Los Alamos, Argentina, and Venice, Italy	Randoll Coate	**90**, 91

Labirinto della Masone, Il	Franco Maria Ricci	199
Fontanellato, Italy		
Labyrinth of Love	Graham Burgess	69
Longleat House, Wiltshire		
Leeds Castle	Adrian Fisher	126, **127**
Leeds, Kent		
Legoland Hedge Maze	Adrian Fisher	145
Legoland Windsor, Berkshire		
Longleat House hedge maze	Greg Bright	64, **65**, 66–7, 200–201
Longleat House, Wiltshire		
Marlborough Maze	Adrian Fisher	142, **143**
Blenheim Palace, Oxfordshire		
New College Worcester [lost]	Anneka Rice	54
Worcester, Worcestershire		
Palace of Versailles [lost]	Charles Perrault	14, **15**
Versailles, France		
Pilton trench maze [lost]	Greg Bright	24–5, 26, **27**, 28, 38–9, 62–3
Worthy Farm, Somerset		
Schloß Schönbrunn [restored]	Jean Trehet	178
Vienna, Austria		
Somerleyton Hall	William Andrews Nesfield	202, **203**
Somerleyton, Suffolk		
Villa Pisani	Girolamo Frigimelica	178
Stra, Italy		
Wyck Rissington Rectory [lost]	Harry Cheales	160, **161**
Wyck Rissington, Gloucestershire		

Flat Mazes

Bellicorum Instrumentorum Liber	Giovanni Fontana	**12**, **13**
paper mazes		
Biblioteca Nazionale Marciana manuscript		76, **77**
(Venice) paper labyrinth		
Bryn Celli Ddu		86–7
pattern stone (Anglesey)		
chakra-vyuh		**138**, 139
labyrinth symbol		

Chartres Cathedral **154**, 155, 157, 162
    (France) pavement labyrinth

'colour maze' Greg Bright 70
    colour maze

Ghost Telepoint Mazes Greg Bright 206–7
    paper mazes

Gotcha Allan Alcorn 43
    video game

Grace Church Cathedral 162–3
    (San Francisco) canvas, tapestry and pavement labyrinths

Hereford Cathedral *mappa mundi* **156**
    paper labyrinth

Hole Maze Greg Bright 71
    paper maze

Labyrinth Mark Wallinger 56, **57**
    (London Underground) maze panels

Libro dei Labirinti Francesco Segala 44
    paper mazes

Mischmasch maze Lewis Carroll **146**, 147
    paper maze

Nazca Lines 196, **197**
    (Peru) geoglyphs

Pac-Man Toru Iwatani 42, 47
    video game

Reims Cathedral 156
    (France) pavement labyrinth

Saffron Walden 176, **177**
    (Essex) turf maze

Scandinavian **35**, 36, 177
    stone labyrinths

'Troy Town' 52
    turf mazes

tshuma sogexe 44
    maze game

Warren Street station Alan Fletcher 44, **45**
    (London Underground) tile maze

Fictional Mazes

Alice's Adventures in Wonderland	Lewis Carroll	5, 147
'Burrow, The'	Franz Kafka	208–9
Disparition, La	Georges Perec	59
'Garden of Forking Paths, The'	Jorge Luis Borges	91
'House of Asterion, The'	Jorge Luis Borges	110–11
Inferno	Dante Alighieri	1, 112–13, 225
King Must Die, The	Mary Renault	172–3
Labyrinth of the World, The	John Amos Comenius	152–3
'Library of Babel, The'	Jorge Luis Borges	30–31
'Little Fable, A'	Franz Kafka	40
Man with the Golden Gun, The	dir. Guy Hamilton	118–19
Maze	Christopher Manson	
Maze, The	William Kurelek (painter)	210–11
Maze Maker, The	Michael Ayrton	4, 12, 136
Maze Runner, The	James Dashner	60
Midsummer Night's Dream, A	William Shakespeare	174–5
'Minotaurus'	Friedrich Dürrenmatt	114–15
Misérables, Les	Victor Hugo	54
Name of the Rose, The	Umberto Eco	22–3, 82, **83**
Pan's Labyrinth	dir. Guillermo del Toro	148–9
Shining, The	dir. Stanley Kubrick	212, **213**
Thésée	André Gide	217
Through the Looking-Glass	Lewis Carroll	158
'Two Kings and the Two Labyrinths, The'	Jorge Luis Borges	199

Mythical Mazes

Caer Sidi	Celtic	87, 132–3
chakra-vyuha	Hindu	78–9
Hell	Christian	126
Knossos	Greek	12, 47, 102–5, 134–5, 190–93
nahal	Vanuatuan	**84**, 85
Rosamund's Bower (Oxfordshire)	English	80–81
Scimangada	Nepalese	53
Tápu'at	Hopi	**140**, 141

Metaphorical Mazes

brains   10, 137, 203–5
breathing   159
cabbages   10
castration   173
caves   2–3, 124, 216
cities   13, 52–8
corals   10
dancing   96, 184–5
death   76–7, 84–5, 87, 128–9
faith   150–51, 155, 159
fingerprints   10
guts   10, 127, 137
honeycombs   4
horsemanship   46–7
life   1, 11, 76, 107, 149, 160, 222–3
love   164–5, 176–9
Mercury, the planet   10
mind, the   202–3, 210–11, 212
mirrors   116–17, 120–21
pilgrimage   150–51, 152, 156–7
quests   41, 57, 58
rebirth   125–7, 129, 140–41, 187
rhizomes   30
shells   10
sun, the   101, 157
traps   33, 34, 36–7, 40, 77, 78–9
underground railways   55–7
universe, the   30–31, 199
whales   10
wombs   7, 137, 138–9
world, the   41, 152–3

Minotaurs

Ayrton, Michael   106
Barye, Antoine-Louis   112–13
Birtwhistle, Harrison   122
Borges, Jorge Luis   99, 110–11
Dürrenmatt, Friedrich   114–15
Frazer, James   100, 101
Gugalanna   v, vii, 98, 99, 100
Man Ray   107
Ovid (Publius Ovidius Naso) 106
Picasso, Pablo   107, 122
Sherrill, Steve   122, 123
Watts, G. F.   110, 111

Henry Eliot grew up playing in the ancient mizmaze on St Catherine's Hill, outside Winchester. His first book, co-written with Matt Lloyd-Rose, was an alternative A to Z of London called *Curiocity*. He is the creative editor of Penguin Classics.

Quibe is a French illustrator and graphic designer based near Paris. Most of his artworks are made with just one line. @quibe